PALESTINE

The Vietnam of Generation Alpha
and the Palestinization of the World

JORGE MAJFUD

HUMANUS

SAN DIEGO-ACAPULCO

Palestine, The Vietnam of Generation Alpha and the Palestinization
of the World
2nd edition with Postscript 2024
© Jorge Majfud 2023
© Illegal Humanus 2023
ISBN: 978-1-956760-97-2
humanus.info
editor@humanus.com

*All author royalties from this book will be donated to child survivors
of the conflict through UN-accredited international organizations*

TABLE OF CONTENTS

The Struggle for Semantic Fields: The Pen and the Rifle 17

Why the Genocide in Gaza is Both Similar to and Different from So Many

Others 21

Hamas Attacks Israel 31

Zionism 35

Anti-Semitism 39

Another Chosen People 45

"We Have the Right to Defend Ourselves Against Terrorists" 51

Our Vietnam 55

The Nazis of Our Time Don't Wear Mustaches 61

Palestine: The Historical (and Strategic) Dehumanization of a People ... 65

Heba Abu Nada Was Murdered Today 71

Google, YouTube and Moralfare 73

By Divine Right 79

The Slow Suicide of the West 87

When the Truth of War Leaks into Our World of Illusions 103

Human Life as Collateral Damage 109

Human Shields 119

Postscript 2024 127

I Have an Illegal Opinion About ████████████ in █████.......................129

What Have We Learned from the Students? 137

The Same Facts. A New Consciousness?...145

Mysteries and Questions of a Neo-Biblical Genocide 153

The Masks of Racism...161

The Mystery of the Palestinian People..167

Olympics of Blood..177

The Empire of Denial Closes Its Eyes and Believes 183

The Ends Justify the Means II 189

Bombs with Much Love 195

Terrorists? 199

The Uncivilized Can Learn to Cultivate the Land 201

Open Letter 209

There Is Something That Cannot Be Bought or Sold, and That's Why It

Bothers So Much 217

1 Samuel 27:7 David lived in Philistine territory for a year and four months. David and his men would raid the Geshurites, the Girzites, and the Amalekites, for these were the ancient inhabitants of the land, from Telam going toward Shur and as far as Egypt.He ravaged the countryside, leaving no man or woman alive; he seized sheep, oxen, donkeys, camels, and garments, then returned to Achish. Achish would ask, "Whom did you raid this time?" David would reply, "The Negev of Judah," or "The territory of the Jerahmeelites," or "The land of the Kenites." David spared no man or woman alive, to avoid bringing them back to Gath, for he said, "Lest they report on us and denounce us to the Philistines." This was David's practice throughout his stay in Philistine territory.

Numbers 31:7-12. So the Israelites fought against Midian, as the Lord had commanded Moses, and killed every male. Among those slain were Midian's five kings—Evi, Rekem, Zur, Hur, and Reba—and they also put Balaam son of Beor to the sword. The Israelites took the Midianite women and children captive, plundered all their livestock, goods, and herds, and burned all their towns and settlements. They gathered all the spoils of war, both people and animals, and brought them to Moses, Eleazar the priest, and the Israelite assembly at their camp on the plains of Moab by the Jordan across from Jericho.

"You must remember what Amalek did to you, says our holy Bible. And we do remember—and we fight."

Benjamin Netanyahu

"BLOT OUT THE MEMORY OF AMALEK. DO NOT FORGET"

Slogan in Hebrew on Israel's Egged buses

"The Zionists wanted all of Palestine served on a silver platter, but it couldn't be done at once. It'll have to be done in small doses. We can't evict six million people and replace them with another six million and expect everyone to be happy."

Harry Truman

"When peace comes, perhaps in time we'll be able to forgive the Arabs for killing our sons, but it will be harder for us to forgive them for forcing us to kill theirs."

Golda Meir, Prime Minister of Israel

"The weapons used to kill Palestinians are American weapons... Hamas was promoted by Israel. We imposed a system on Palestinians to let them democratically elect their leaders. But since the people chose the party we promoted, now we have to kill them."

Ron Paul, Texas Congressman

"We have many wealthy Americans who want to come populate Gaza. I have five hundred in my phone contacts. Two million Arabs will leave Gaza and we will occupy it. They want to annihilate the State of Israel. They're monsters. Yes, you can call it ethnic cleansing if you want."

Daniella Weiss, settler leader

"Letting two million Palestinians starve to death in Gaza would be justified and moral."

Bezalel Smotrich, Israeli Finance Minister

"Our actions are guided by the Torah. Everything is written here. It says wherever there's a Jewish settlement, there will be security. Why would it be immoral to take land from someone who wants to kill me? My ancestors lived there."

Amihai Elyahu, Heritage Minister

"We killed thousands of Amalekites... Morally, every Arab is suspect! We have no morality. Being moral is killing all terrorists after interrogating them... Being moral is razing and conquering all of Israel."

Chai Ben Hamo, Israeli soldier and rabbi

"Israeli society has surrounded itself with physical and mental walls. Most Israelis, if not all, are convinced we are the chosen people and therefore have the right to do as we please. Israeli colonization is the only one I know in history where the occupier plays the victim... Golda Meir herself said that after the Holocaust, Jews can do whatever they want. The worst part is that the dehumanization of Palestinians is what allows Israelis to live peacefully with our conscience. If they're not human like us, then it's not a human rights issue. I once asked Minister Ehud Barak what he would have done if he were

Palestinian. 'I would have joined a terrorist group,' he told me... Once I encountered an ambulance stopped for an hour. I confronted the soldiers playing backgammon, asking if they'd do the same if their parents were in that ambulance. They became furious because I dared compare their parents to a Palestinian."

Gideon Levy, Israeli journalist and writer

"The enemy isn't Hamas. Every child, every baby in Gaza is an enemy. Not a single Palestinian child should remain there."

Moshe Feiglin, Israeli parliament member

"What? Gaza still exists? Then why did you wake me? Oh, we erased it? Let me know when nothing's left."

Moshe Korsia, Israeli soldier and artist

"I have no pity for Gazans. I don't believe there's anyone in the State of Israel, in the Land of Israel, who should feel sorry for them. Not for adults, not for elders, not for youth, not for children. Gazans can starve to death. What do I care? Why should we worry about them?"

Yaki Adamker, Israeli journalist.

"Why are we spending our money to build them a port? We shouldn't spend a single coin on humanita-rian aid. It should be like Hiroshima and Nagasaki and end this quickly."

Tim Walberg, U.S. Congressman

"The 'settler violence' campaign is an antisemitic lie spread by Israel's enemies to discredit pioneering settlers and the settlement enterprise, harm them, and thus discredit the entire State of Israel. This is an immoral boycott campaign against Israel, one that turns the victim into the aggressor and allows settlers' blood to be spilled. It's shameful that a government would cooperate with this during days when settlers are paying with their lives in the Gaza war. With God's help, I will continue acting courageously to strengthen and develop Jewish settlements across the Land of Israel and fight for sustainable peace, which can only be achieved when Arabs' hope of establishing an Arab state on the ruins of the Jewish state fades away. If the price is U.S. sanctions imposed against me, so be it."

Bezalel Smotrich, Israeli Finance Minister

"If you support genocide, you don't get arrested—you get applauded."

Medea Benjamin, Jewish activist against genocide in Palestine

"There are no innocents in Gaza, no such thing exists. In Gaza, everyone is guilty, everyone chose Hamas, everyone over 4 years old is a Hamas sympathizer."

Rami Igra, Mossad Director

"The word *apartheid* is the most accurate to describe Palestine... I don't want to converse even indirectly with Dershowitz. I have no need to debate someone unfamiliar with Palestine's situation... In the U.S., nothing critical of Israel is debated."

Jimmy Carter

"The genocide in Gaza is not in my name."

Stephen Kapos, Holocaust survivor

"Jews don't have to play by the world's rules because the world is immoral. The world has a twisted notion of morality... The land of Israel belongs to us because the God of Abraham, Isaac, and Jacob gave it to us. God created the entire world and on that day decided to give this land to the Jews... When we start speaking the language of the Torah, the world will begin respecting us. The world doesn't want us to follow its rules... The world gets furious when we try to resemble them. They want us at the head of the class. They want us to lead and teach them. Soon they'll be begging us, 'Jews, please show us the way.' Then we can't make the same mistake again by talking about democracy. We must speak as what we are: God's chosen people. Some presume to teach morality to Jews, when we were the ones who brought morality to the world. We must clarify that we are God's chosen and the protagonists of the greatest story ever told. So gentlemen, a little more respect and humility, and we'll be delighted to show you the way."

Berel Solomon, Israeli activist and motivator

"Some education is needed. When we speak of crimes against humanity and war crimes, it's not a matter of degrees but of essence. When a bomb causes collateral damage, Palestinian children will undoubtedly die. But those children won't die feeling betrayed by humanity. What's horrific here is imagining Israeli children dying with that last image of inhumanity.

I believe we must explain this because in the world of emotions, incomparable things are being compared."

Céline Pina, French journalist

"We are fighting human animals."

Yoav Gallant, Israeli Defense Minister

"In the (Jewish) community where I grew up, we didn't just blame the perpetrators of the Holocaust. We also blamed the passive witnesses to genocide, those who simply looked away and let it happen. That's why I fight against this genocide (in Palestine), because it's a Crime Against Humanity. It's a crime against all of us. This isn't a religious conflict. Jews, Christians, and Muslims lived in peace for millennia in Palestine, in Jerusalem. It was only with the arrival of Zionists that conflict erupted, and that conflict wasn't just Zionists against Palestinians. It was also Zionists against Jews and Zionists against Christians. So right now, basic education is desperately needed. Israel's apartheid government must end the ethnic cleansing. This didn't begin on October 7th. This has been the history since before Israel's founding."

Jill Stein, U.S. presidential candidate

"Saying a state (like Israel) has a right to exist makes no sense. States don't have rights. Human beings have rights."

Aviva Chomsky, historian and activist

"Personally, I'm proud of Gaza's ruins. All the babies, even 80 years from now, will tell their grandchildren what the Jews did."

May Golan, Israeli Minister for the Advancement of Women

Two Palestinian children beside their mother's body.
Gaza, November 2023

THE BATTLE OVER SEMANTICS: THE PEN AND THE RIFLE

ON ONE SIDE, THERE ARE HISTORICAL FACTS that everyone, more or less, knows. On the other hand, there is something far more important: the dialectical struggle and the narrative war. In other words: psychological warfare.

In the case of the Gaza Massacre, this divides into two groups: (1) one group insists through its rhetoric (or through facts) that *not all human beings are equal*. It is a medieval, pre-Enlightenment conviction. Back then, the mere idea that a noble's life and a peasant's life held equal value provoked unanimous laughter, even among peasants. The other group (2) insists on the humanist principle that all lives have equal worth. Ironically, it is the latter who are accused of being racist and supporting terrorism.

Humanism and the Enlightenment introduced the consensus (the idea existed vaguely among ancient Greeks and early Christians) that every life is equally valuable. This notion, once absurd, became a paradigm. But in practice, it continues to be proven that not all lives hold equal value. The phrase "all men are created equal," refined in the U.S. Declaration of Independence, was simultaneously a theoretical truth and a practical lie. Those who wrote it believed in the superiority of "the white race," were slaveholders, and never ceased to be so.

Although the oppressed have managed to secure (always by force or through some unequal struggle against entrenched power) many rights based on the principle of equality, the evidence of reality has not changed much. When in January 2015 a terrorist group murdered 12 people in Paris, a dozen world leaders—from Nicolas Sarkozy, François Hollande, and Angela Merkel to Benjamin Netanyahu and Mahmoud Abbas—marched arm in arm through Paris' streets. At the front of that march walked Mali's president, Ibrahim Keita, and Nigeria's president, Mahamadou Issoufou. The world rallied under the slogan "Je suis Charlie."

Almost simultaneously, Boko Haram was massacring hundreds in Nigeria, following other mass killings in that same country the previous year, with an estimated 6,000 victims. There were no marches. No tears. The press barely reported it. They were Black and, perhaps worse than that, they were poor and lived in one of those "shithole countries," in the words of President Donald Trump.

The many hundreds of millions of dead from Western empires are scarcely mentioned in history books, let alone in major media.

WHY IS THE GENOCIDE IN GAZA BOTH THE SAME AND DIFFERENT FROM SO MANY OTHERS?

THE DEFENDERS OF THE GENOCIDE IN PALESTINE argue that it is not a genocide and that, furthermore, there have been other genocides just as bad or worse in recent history. From dehumanizing the victims massacred under bombs or executed daily with absolute impunity, they move on to threatening and criminalizing their critics. The traditional method is to accuse them of antisemitism and then blacklist them so they lose their jobs or get expelled from their countries of residence, as has happened many times. One of the extortion services, aside from the nearly infinite resources of the CIA and Mossad, consists of various harassment archives, like the most recently acknowledged by the U.S. government, *doxing* Canary Mission (in this case, to criminalize students and professors critical of Israel), along with a multitude of actions that will one day be revealed in greater detail through leaks or declassified documents, as often happens—and in which we will discover names, both of critics and activists listed for extortion and civil death, as well as mercenary and voluntary collaborators, those who freely offer themselves to punish honest individuals through the world's greatest powers, because their mediocrity and cowardice never allowed them to do so on their own merits—some of whose names we already know.

Of course, there have been other genocides in history. In the case of the Modern Era, most—and the worst—genocides that claimed millions of victims, intentionally or systematically eliminated, were perpetrated or heavily supported by the great Northwestern empires. We have written about this years ago.

Take, for example, one of the worst genocides of recent generations: the Rwandan genocide. For three months, Rwanda's Hutu militias, protected by Jean Kambanda's government, massacred Tutsis and even some members of their own Hutu ethnicity caught in the middle. As could only be expected, this genocide was fueled and directed by the far-right ideology of Hutu Supremacy, who considered themselves racially superior to Tutsis and, consequently, entitled to erase them from the face of the Earth. To justify their ancestral claim to the land, the Hutus invoked myths about a pre-existing Hutu population in Rwanda before the arrival of Tutsis from Ethiopia. They then imposed apartheid in key state institutions like education and the military. Next, they criminalized any Hutu who befriended a Tutsi or dared to defend their humanity. Studies on these Bantu peoples show genetic and ethnic differences that are negligible compared to neighboring groups.

In May 1994, the UN imposed an arms embargo on the supremacist, genocidal government of Kambanda and his defense minister Théoneste Bagosora. This embargo was violated by France and Apartheid South Africa in its final months. In June, coinciding with Nelson Mandela's rise to power in South Africa, UN peacekeepers entered Rwanda, and the genocide ended in less than a month. Years later, Bill Clinton expressed regret for doing nothing to stop this genocide, despite the fact that Washington's interventions—like Europe's—never asked anyone's permission. In fact, he did do something: the UN Security Council ordered the withdrawal of peacekeeping forces before the genocide, and Washington refused to use the word "genocide" while the slaughter continued unrestricted, despite protests from humanitarian groups worldwide, including military figures like Canadian General Roméo Dallaire.

Approximately half a million Tutsis were killed with the intention of being annihilated as a people or removed from their lands for the benefit of the dominant ethnic group. That is, a figure comparable to what is estimated in the case of Palestine in just the last few years, not even accounting for the first Nakba from 1946 to 1948 and the constant war against Palestinians in Palestine that, since then and without respite, has left an average of 1,500 Palestinians dead per year—aside from those dispossessed of their lands and human rights by armed settlers, and aside from those kidnapped by the Israeli military itself, including thousands of children.

The difference between the genocide in Gaza and other genocides where hundreds of thousands were similarly killed is clear.

Although the supremacist ideology of Hutu Power had been fermenting for many years, the genocide in Rwanda occurred within a span of three months.

Neither its ideologues nor those who carried it out spent every day, every year, and decade after decade sermonizing in the world's most powerful media outletsto ensure no one acknowledged that a genocide was being committed in Rwanda.

No one in the world repeated the excuse of Hutu Supremacy that Rwanda had the right to defend itself, much less that massacring children, men, and women of all ages every day was part of that right.

Unlike the Zionists, the Hutu supremacists did not have star journalists in major news channels and media outlets worldwide, commenting on the news with a Rwandan flag on their desks, justifying violence against Tutsis and criminalizing their resistance as anti-Bantu terrorists.

Apart from the Hutus in Rwanda, no group or church in Berlin, Atlanta, São Paulo, Buenos Aires, Lagos, or New Delhi justified the Hutus or prayed for their safety, despite them being Christians.

Prime Minister Jean Kambanda did not travel to Washington to give speeches in Congress. He did not receive standing ovations from lawmakers supporting his supremacist project to pass laws criminalizing defenders of Tutsi rights in the West or imposing loyalty oaths to Rwandaas a requirement for holding public office or receiving aid in the face of climate disasters.

Kambanda was not received by every U.S. president to secure trillions of dollars in financial, military, media, and moral support.

Hutu Supremacy did not have the most powerful lobby in the West funding every winning politician in the U.S., nor did representatives of the people have Rwandan flags at the entrances to their offices. No one, like Senator Rafael (Ted) Cruz and so many others, declared that their primary mission in Washington was to protect Rwanda.

Neither Théoneste Bagosora nor Hutu Supremacy were unconditionally supported by the majority of European countries or by the President of the European Commission, even though Europe had killed more millions of Africans in Africa than Jews in the Holocaust during World War II and should, by the same logic, feel remorse at least as profound for African peoples as for Jewish and Romani peoples.

Neither Americans, Germans, nor Argentinians who displayed Tutsi flags were arrested and beaten by the police in their civilized countries, norwere they accused of inciting anti-Bantu hatred, even though both Hutus and Tutsis are Bantu peoples.

No U.S. president threatened from the White House to kidnap and send to a concentration camp in El Salvador all those who criticized Rwanda, because criticizing Rwanda was deemed anti-American.

Governors in the U.S. did not send directives to university professors forbidding them from using words likegenocide,Tutsi, orHutu supremacy. They did not ask students to record professors, nor did the federal government use masked agents to kidnap students off the streets for writing articles defending the human rights of Tutsis.

Professors of Moral Philosophy or African Studies did not cancel their courses on Tutsi History or Human Rights in Rwanda for fear of losing their jobs—whether through dismissal, contract termination in violation of *tenure* regulations, arbitrary salary cuts, or the fear of never finding employment elsewhere once fired.

Not even South African apartheid had the power to dictate to presidents and senators of theworld's greatest powers, like Europe and the U.S., what they should say and do.

The Rwandan génocidaires did not own the world's largest financial capitals like BlackRock, JPMorgan, or Barclays. They had no dealings with major surveillance and public opinion manipulation tech firms like Palantir. They did not decide dozens of elections worldwide, like Team Jorge. They did not have the most powerful and lethal intelligence agency in the world, nor did they collaborate with the other two largest intelligence agencies.

Jean Kambanda was not in power for three decades but three months—and was tried and convicted of genocide. His ministers, military officers, Hutu supremacist ideologues, and journalists were also sentenced to decades in prison for genocide, crimes

against humanity, incitement, or apology for genocide.

Repugnant as any other genocide, the Rwandan
genocide was neither the cause nor the consequence
of a systematic*Rwandanization* of the world, where debate and dissent were replaced by violence and the
politics of cruelty.

Because of power's deafening harassment.
Because of bombers' blind rationality.
Because of the triumph of racism, xenophobia and sex-
ism.
Because of love's prostitution.
Because of hate's commercialization.
Because of the fear to exist and to feel.
Because of the fear to think differently.
Because of tribalism's dopamine and blood's metallic
taste.
Because of the manipulation of ideas and emotions.
Because of social engineering through hunger.
Because of need as an instrument of control.
Because of voluntary slavery.
Because of religious fanaticism.
Because of mass indoctrination.
Because of the illusion of individual freedom.
Because of the sanctification of the most powerful.

Because of the criminalization of the weakest.
Because of police militarization.
Because of justice's politicization.
Because of the whip that educates the slave.
Because of admiration for the slaver.

Because of the psychopath's law—unable to distinguish good from evil, replacing morality with the only thing that stirs emotion: winning or losing.

The Rwandan genocide happened in Rwanda. The genocide in Palestine happens in Gaza—and in every office, on every street corner, in every bedroom across the world.

HAMAS ATTACKS ISRAEL

ACCORDING TO A MINOR NOTE in The Washington Post, between January and September 2023, 227 Palestinians were killed by Israeli military forces and settlers—who, with impunity, routinely evict Palestinians from their homes and farms. When they don't kill them, they kidnap them under any accusation based on soldiers' discretion and Israeli law. These 227 deaths went unnoticed. No marches, no media outrage, no condemnation from the world's powerful leaders. They never mattered. They were *nobodies*, they were animals, they were numbers, they were *nothing*.

After the tragic October 7 (followed by many far more *tragic* days that won't necessarily be labeled as such), those who from the start condemned both Hamas's militant actions and the Israeli government's have been accused of "supporting terrorism" by those who only condemn Hamas while justifying the Israeli government's massive, historical, and systematic terrorism.

That the world's most heavily guarded border could be invaded by a group of rudimentary terrorists—and that the response from the world's fourth-

most powerful military took hours—is as unbelieva-
ble as the claim that, 22 years earlier, Saudi aviation
students brought down the world's two most heavily
guarded towers by hijacking commercial planes from
the world's most heavily guarded airports. Beyond the
delayed reaction, when Israeli pilots in super-ad-
vanced jets with super-technology couldn't distinguish Hamas terrorists from their own citizens. Weeks
later, in a pretense of objective honesty, Israel's government admitted the death toll was 200 fewer than
reported—having initially counted charred foreign
bodies as their own, an implicit admission of indiscriminate bombing by their own air force, which
failed to recognize their own citizens as victims of foreign terrorists. Israel's military claims to know everything about tunnels beneath hospitals it mercilessly
bombs, yet knew nothing about Hamas militants
crossing for hostages...

Then came the brutal "counterterrorism defense"
response—leaving over 11,000 massacred innocents,
nearly half children (notably, almost half of Gaza's
population is underage), not counting the thousands
buried under rubble or the two million innocents suffering the most severe Post-Traumatic Stress Disorder
(PTSD) imaginable. A breeding ground for "terrorists," if there ever was one.

Entire areas are bombed, including hospitals, schools and refugee camps, under the excuse that terrorists might be there. Israeli intelligence—which failed to foresee or prevent Hamas's brief October 7 invasion—claims to know everything happening in Palestine's underground. The blame for so many Palestinian children dying falls on Hamas terrorists using them as shields. As the famed Prime Minister Golda Meir summarized half a century ago: "We can never forgive the Arabs for forcing us to kill their children." This is the genocidal, deeply terrorist logic we've reached in the name of (1) God, (2) democracy, (3) self-defense, and (4) the war on terror.

Right now, beyond the unilateral principle of "the right to defend itself," pro-Israel demands focus on freeing hostages still held by Hamas—something we openly support. But why don't we also talk about Israel's systematic kidnapping of Palestinians? Thousands languish in Israeli prisons without trial, accused of insulting or disobeying soldiers' arbitrary orders. Or for throwing stones at the fourth most powerful army in the world. Israeli ambassador Gilad Erdan himself, in a speech at the UN, held up a brick to demonstrate Palestinian aggression. How far can a child, or an adult, throw such a concrete block with one hand? Many of those imprisoned are minors—

effectively kidnapped by a foreign state, like the recent case of young Ahed Tamimi, along with 7,000 other Palestinian hostages who aren't called such to avoid offending the sensibilities of the civilized, democratic West.

Now, let's set aside the historical contingencies of the present moment and focus on the core concepts of this conflict, which is not just regional but global— both in its causes and consequences.

ZIONISM

ZIONISM ORIGINATED in 17th-century imperial England. Its promoters were Protestant Christians who believed Jesus' second coming would occur in 1666, following the return of the Hebrew people to Palestine and their acceptance of Jesus as the Messiah. That is, after the Jews converted to Christianity. Nothing new.

According to Israeli historian and Zionism expert Anita Shapira from Tel Aviv University, evangelical Zionists transmitted this idea to some Jewish communities in the mid-19th century, despite resistance from rabbis themselves against Jewish nationalism since the early 1800s. Current statistics show Zionism today consists of one Jew for every thirty Christians.

The primary opponents of Zionism, from its inception, were Jews. They still are. While Palestinians have come to accept a two-state solution, anti-Zionist Orthodox Jews demand the dismantling of *the entire* State of Israel, which they consider anti-Jewish. For them, the "return of the Hebrew people" to their land isn't a political act and certainly not a military one, but a miracle from God. As a popular saying goes,

"Zionists don't believe in God, but they're certain He gave them the land."

Today, one such anti-Zionist Jewish group is Neturei Karta, founded in Jerusalem in 1938. At the time, Hitler supported the Zionist idea as a form of voluntary ethnic cleansing—similar to what happened with Black Americans after Lincoln granted them voting rights: many were "sent back" to Haiti and Africa, where they founded Liberia. This resembles what Netanyahu and his apologists want for the inconvenient Palestinian population: for them to leave, to seek refuge elsewhere. In fact, the Palestinian diaspora, numbering around ten million, has exceeded Palestine's native population for over two decades.

Other anti-Zionist Orthodox Jews live north of Jerusalem in Mea Shearim, a neighborhood I visited in the 90s when peace between Jews and Palestinians seemed possible. Days after I left Palestine and Israel (following two hours of interrogation at Tel Aviv airport), a far-right fanatic assassinated Prime Minister Yitzhak Rabin, achieving his goal of destroying any hope for coexistence.

Just as 4th-century Christians transformed from persecuted to persecutors under Emperor Constantine's brutal patronage, Jews—persecuted, expelled, and demonized by Christians in Europe for centuries—became persecutors after World War II.

In 1975, the UN General Assembly declared in Resolution 3379 that "Zionism is a form of racism and racial discrimination." This was revoked in 1991 as a condition for Israel's participation in the Madrid Peace Conference, which led to the Oslo Accords. A decade later, these accords also failed, as illegal settlements proliferated contrary to all promises of Palestinian independence.

The Jewish people survived two millennia in diaspora across Asia, Africa, Europe, and the Americas. Expelled and persecuted dozens of times, especially in Europe and the U.S. before 1945, their spirit remained unshaken—until the State of Israel succeeded in breaking it.

ANTISEMITISM

THROUGHOUT MOST OF THE 20TH CENTURY, especially after the Holocaust and Israel's creation, accusations of "antisemitism" became among the most feared labels for critics of Israeli government policies. This absurdity stems from the strategic conflation of Zionism and Judaism. Similarly, all nationalisms have hijacked diverse peoples by equating *their* political decisions with an entire country. In wartime, any criticism was—and is—seen as unpatriotic, reduced to the vulgar, criminal dichotomy of "them or us."

Benjamin Netanyahu justifies land ownership through a mystical ethno-racial lineage spanning over two millennia. Opponents are branded *antisemitic*—a racial or at least ethnic slur. Ironically, Netanyahu and most Israelis are less *Semitic* than Palestinians. Modern Israelis are as Semitic as Zionists are religious. Genetic studies show roughly half of Jewish ancestry traces to the ancient Middle East, the other half to Europe.

Palestinians aren't just more Semitic than Israelis—they're genetically the closest group to modern Jews. Yet Netanyahu's government officials have called them "two-legged animals," and many Israelis view them as inhuman beasts or at least an inferior caste—subjected to physical and moral violence far worse than India's untouchables. What could be more antisemitic than this today? It's the old strategy the Nazis used against Jews in Europe: first dehumanize them, call them *rats*; then exterminate, as one exterminates rats. None of this is considered antisemitism—the Devil only knows why.

Yet another tragic paradox. This conflation of Judaism with Semitism and with the State of Israel has discredited (when not outright criminalized) leftist movements worldwide, making them the primary target of antisemitism accusations. Any humanist stance that sees no difference in worth or rights between Palestinian and Israeli lives—and openly protests as such—is automatically labeled as *antisemitism*.

This is the absurdity we've reached. Simultaneously, far-right factions have become bastions of pro-Israel sentiment. Consider the American far-right with its white supremacism, including various neo-Nazi groups—historically champions of antisemitism. Or Brazil's far-right, like the clan of former President Bolsonaro, obsessed with Israeli flags and their evangelical cause—everything returns to its origin. Or Argentina's ultra-right presidential candidate Javier

Milei, waving Israeli flags at his political rallies. Or, at a time when millions march globally protesting the Gaza massacre, Paris witnesses Marine Le Pen—historic leader of France's neo-Nazi and fascist far-right—and Jordan Bardella, president of the far-right National Rally party, organizing a march "against antisemitism" targeting those who dare denounce the brutality of the world's fourth most powerful army against defenseless civilians.

A paradox is an apparent contradiction with underlying rigid logic. Of course, the current panic among declining empires isn't exclusive to the far-right. Céline Pina, parliamentary assistant in France's Senate and militant of the *Parti Socialiste* (PS), who in 2016 compared Islamic veils to Nazi armbands, naturally took sides in the Gaza conflict. Her reasoning mirrors all Western empires that devastated and murdered hundreds of millions of Asians, Africans, and Latin Americans—always in civilization's name, for the Free World, and once more against the invasion of inferior races: "*a bomb that explodes, destroys, and causes collateral damage will undoubtedly kill (Palestinian) children. But these children won't die feeling humanity betrayed them. They died being everything they had the right to expect to be. What's horrific here is imagining the (Israeli) children aged 8, 9, 10, those poor women dying with their last image being one of inhumanity, atrocity, and contempt for who they were. That's where the crime against humanity lies.*" All panelists accompanying her on French TV agreed.

According to physicist Hajo Meyer, Auschwitz survivor and anti-Zionist Jew: "Israeli schools teach racism against Palestinians, indoctrinating about state, blood, and soil—just as Nazis taught me in Germany. Zionism is a nationalist, racist, colonialist ideology." In 2006, Meyer was accused of antisemitism in Germany for comparing Israel's occupation of Palestinian territories to the Nazi regime.

ANOTHER CHOSEN PEOPLE

ACCORDING TO A PEW survey, 70% of Israelis believe they're God's chosen people. 17% don't even believe in God. Of course, this selection supposedly occurred millennia ago, but judging by beliefs and policies enforced via F-35 Lightning fighter jets, this preference appears hereditary. The same surveys show 17% of Israelis are atheists—but that's just a detail.

The notion of being a chosen people differs little from considering oneself a prophet chosen by God— or even God's child. Yet morally and sociologically, their preachings and practices show abysmal differences.

Let's analyze this. The prophet concept dominating Western culture stems from Greek roots: a prophet predicts the future. In the Old Testament, prophets had nothing to do with this. A prophet was someone who fearlessly, without flattery, dared to point out their people's moral sins. Prophets like Amos openly criticized ruling-class greed and social injustice's immorality. For much of Christian tradition, Jesus is God's Son—but it's easy to view him similarly. Jesus too was a prophet who spared no criticism of his people's moral failings and hypocrisy. He was executed like a common criminal alongside two other outlaws by the empire and local collaborators of the time.

Now, his claim of divinity was considered supremely arrogant—just as a people considering themselves "God's chosen" remains arrogant. This idea originates in Deuteronomy, the Torah's fifth book, when Egyptian Moses prepared his people to enter the Promised Land. This book was actually written centuries after Canaan's violent conquest.

However, in Jesus' case, his claim didn't translate into special rights to oppress others—quite the opposite. Beyond advocating democratic, indiscriminate love (including loving one's enemies), Jesus claimed to have come to sacrifice himself for others' sins. Myth or reality, this idea is neither egocentric nor genocidal—quite the contrary.

The problem arises when the arrogance of being *God's chosen people* implies *special rights*—and moreover, the right to oppress another people. A pretense that, historically speaking, isn't particularly special or exclusive.

This notion of being "God's chosen people" has been standard in the nationalist self-narratives of numerous other cultures. For instance, Huitzilopochtli, the warrior god of the Mexica (later Aztecs), commanded his chosen people to undertake an exodus southward in search of the Promised Land. Wherever they saw an eagle killing a snake atop a cactus by a lake, they were to take possession. Naturally, this land was already inhabited, requiring the application of divine eviction mandates under the conviction that they were the *chosen people*.

On another continent—to avoid excessive detail—the traditional religion of East Africa's Maasai people holds that the supreme and only god, Ngai, chose them to herd all the world's cattle. Predictably, this belief has been used to justify cattle theft from other tribes.

Even accepting the unacceptable (that one people might have special rights over others by being chosen by their own god), one could still ask: Does being chosen by God confer the right to oppress and decide for others? Is the Universe's Creator some nationalist barbarian who hates the rest of His own creation?

According to the 1988 "Statement of Principles of Conservative Judaism" by the Rabbinical Assembly at New York's United Synagogue, being God's chosen people "far from being a license for special privilege, implies additional responsibilities—not only toward God but toward our fellow humans... It obligates us to build a just and compassionate society worldwide, especially in the land of Israel."

I know of no case where a people created a religion declaring their neighbors as God's chosen. That Caucasian Christians did so stemmed from their religion emerging from the same Hebrew texts. Naturally, they wouldn't renounce the ancestral canon of considering themselves the elect. Christianity appropriated this divine preference by demonizing the original chosen people—herein lies real antisemitism.

In a 1981 interview, mythologist Joseph Campbell called the chosen people idea "an anachronistic myth from another era" where the hero assumes collective form. He was accused of antisemitism.

"WE HAVE THE RIGHT TO DEFEND OURSELVES AGAINST TERRORISTS"

THIS RIGHT DOESN'T EXTEND to the occupied but to the occupiers. As Israeli journalist Gideon Levy noted, "I know no occupying force in history that presented itself as victims of the occupied."

Israel's Heritage Minister Amichai Eliyahu disagrees: "Anyone waving a Palestinian flag shouldn't continue living on this planet." Days earlier, he'd proposed nuking Gaza, despite Israel's insistence that it either lacks such weapons or doesn't know how many it possesses.

The UN declaration (General Assembly Resolution 37/43, 1982) recognizes and "*reaffirms the legitimacy of peoples' struggle for independence, territorial integrity, national unity and liberation from colonial/foreign domination by all available means, including armed struggle*". Yet any native resistance, any Palestinian resistance, is invariably branded "terrorist" by dominant media—precisely the label the U.S. and Britain applied for decades to Nelson Mandela and the ANC for sabotaging South Africa's apartheid, that racist oppressive regime Ronald Reagan called in 1982 "an ally of the Free World". Mandela himself, visiting Gaza in

1999, was clear about his anti-apartheid struggle: "we must choose peace over confrontation—except when there's no alternative; then, if violence is the only option, we'll use violence."

Don't Palestinians have the right to armed self-defense? Why not? Israel's government claims Gaza's 11,000 dead civilians (so far) aren't innocent. That bombing hospitals is justified by Hamas tunnels beneath them, even asserting "there are no innocents." Why couldn't Hamas say the same, especially given Israelis' compulsory military service and AK-47s carried even during shopping trips to their pristine *malls*?

To humanists, this depressing logic applies equally on either side of that cursed border. A basic principle holds that a law is moral only when claimed for ourselves and extended to others. Not so for fanatics claiming special rights as God's chosen. Not so for powers daily unleashing untouchable brutality on "two-legged animals." When those animals resist, it's terrorism; when critics question this genocidal logic, they're demonized as "antisemites" or "terror apologists." Beyond state terrorism, this is psychological and media terrorism wielded across modernity's senile empires.

For racist fanatics, "we're special." We're "true humans," while "Palestinians are animals" to be exterminated. This is not an interpretation. Israeli Prime Minister Benjamin Netanyahu stated it explicitly in one of his televised messages, quoting a people destroyed two and a half millennia ago according to biblical tradition, the Amalekites: "*Go, attack Amalek, and utterly destroy all that they have; do not spare them, but kill both man and woman, child and infant, ox and sheep, camel and donkey*" (1 Samuel 15:3). Biblical scholars maintain that Amalek never existed, but for our purposes this is an irrelevant detail. As should be almost all arguments based on religious manipulations to establish the International Law of some peoples to oppress others.

OUR VIETNAM

SHORTLY AFTER THE long-desired destruction of Gaza began under a prime minister besieged by corruption allegations and accusations of judicial and parliamentary coup, Netanyahu warned Iran on television: "the best thing you can do is remain silent."

Where does this geopolitical arrogance come from if not from the military and financial power still structured around the ancient order of dying modern empires? During the first days of the new Palestinian massacre, the West released $16 billion in frozen Iranian funds held in the United States, to ensure that country wouldn't interfere in what doesn't concern it.

There are many other exogenous reasons behind the tragedy of thousands of massacred children in Gaza alone. One unproven speculation (which I consider somewhat weak) suggests Israel wants to revive the Ben Gurion Canal project. This project was studied and detailed in the 1950s and aimed to connect northern Gaza to the Red Sea using atomic bombs, to compete with the Suez Canal after its nationalization by Gamal Abdel Nasser in 1956 - which sparked a prolonged conflict. At that time, Britain, France and Israel attacked Egypt to regain control of the canal.

According to Netanyahu, the current plan to connect Gaza's northern border to the Red Sea would actually be a high-speed rail line. Who knows.

Another speculation, with more factual support, points to the discovery of gas and oil off Gaza's coast. Even more plausible is the explanation by current Democratic White House candidate Robert Kennedy Jr.: "Israel is a bulwark for us... it's almost like having an aircraft carrier in the Middle East. If Israel disappears, Russia, China and the BRICS will control 90% of the world's oil, which would be a catastrophe for U.S. national security." The strength of this argument lies in its sufficiency.

Months earlier we mentioned a "geopolitical earthquake" that went unreported by major media. One needn't be clever to see that the geopolitical power shift from West to East will bring multiple realignments and conflicts, from Africa and Latin America to the currently forgotten NATO war in Ukraine. The Israeli-Palestinian conflict has been key for nearly a century and will become even more so.

It's highly likely that U.S., European and Israeli intelligence services have this hot data on their desks. I doubt there's even minimal room for uncertainty. Declassified documents from this period (if any remain) will reveal the most urgent idea and objective:

the world will be much harder to manipulate in our favor by 2040; so let's do what we can while we still can, or abandon our goals forever. Among these urgent priorities is the use and abuse of dollar creation before the green currency is abandoned as global reserve and safe haven. Before the monetary abuse initiated by Richard Nixon in 1971 generates even worse hyperinflation than the 1970s, in the country that issues and manages monetary fiction to keep others in perpetual debt and production.

The Israeli-Palestinian conflict is another of these urgent objectives before losing absolute control. In other words, we're facing multiple "final solutions" scenarios, like Germany losing WWII, but on a much larger scale and over longer timeframes. As a solution to Gaza's humanitarian crisis, Israel shamelessly proposes that Palestinians surviving the massacre be received as refugees in other countries, confirming the original plan to ethnically cleanse the area of those inconvenient animals.

As usual, rigged polls sell like hotcakes. Manipulators don't just hack public opinion - when it doesn't meet expectations, they hack the results. Some remain more reliable due to transparent methodology. A 2021 poll by the Jewish Electorate Institute (JEI) among Jewish voters showed a quarter agreed Israel is an apartheid state. By 2023, according to Pew, most American Jews didn't support unconditional aid to Israel and would only back the billions Washington sends yearly to Tel Aviv if it wasn't used to promote occupation of Palestinian territories. As the saying goes, the road to hell is paved with good intentions.

In response to the ongoing Gaza massacre, various Jewish groups organized protest marches against Israel's brutality. Dozens demonstrating in New York against Gaza's 10,000+ deaths were arrested. Other members of *Jews For Ceasefire* were arrested protesting outside Chicago's Israeli consulate. These groups include anti-Zionist Hasidic Jews.

Palestine will be the new generation's Vietnam in the West. Like Vietnam, it won't alter global geopolitics - that will follow other paths - but it will change how a generation perceives dominant narratives. Radical change will take longer and emerge with the new geopolitical balance (or imbalance) starting mid-century. If anything, sooner.

THE NAZIS OF OUR TIME DON'T WEAR MUSTACHES

IT REMAINS A TRAGIC IRONY OF HISTORY that those who from the beginning condemned the warlike actions of Hamas and the Israeli government are accused of supporting *terrorism* by those who only condemn Hamas while justifying the massive, historical and systematic terrorism of the Israeli government.

Fortunately, hundreds of thousands of Jews (particularly in the northern hemisphere) have shown the courage lacking in politically correct and predictable evangelicals and secularists by taking to the streets and centers of global power to clarify that *the State of Israel and Judaism are not the same thing* - a basic, strategic and functional confusion at the heart of this conflict that benefits only a few through the fanatical and ignorant complicity of many others.

In fact, tens of thousands of Jews well-versed in sacred Jewish texts like the Torah have affirmed that Judaism is anti-Zionist. Many will say this is a matter of opinion, but I see no reason why their opinion should carry less weight than that of other warmongering charlatans.

It has been these Jews, who know their coexistence with Muslims was for centuries far better than this modern tragedy, who have shouted in Washington and New York "Not in our name," "Stop the Apartheid genocide," and who in not few cases have been arrested for exercising their freedom of speech - a freedom that in imperial democracies has always belonged only to those unimportant enough to challenge political power, as demonstrated by free speech during slavery times. But history will grant dignity to these protesters.

When light returns to Gaza and the world learns what one of the most powerful nuclear armies, with Europe and America's complicity, has done to a defenseless ghetto and a people entitled to nothing but breathing when possible - we'll discover not thousands but tens of thousands of lives as valuable as our own, crushed by the racist, mechanical hatred of sick individuals, a few of whom wield tremendous political, geopolitical, media and financial power - which is ultimately what rules the world. Naturally, commercial propaganda will try to deny it. History won't. It will be merciless, as always when the victims no longer inconvenience anyone.

Many will stay silent, trembling at the consequences - blacklists (jobless journalists, students without scholarships, politicians without donations, as even outlets like the New York Times have reported), the social stigma endured by those daring to say there are no chosen peoples or individuals - neither by God nor Devil - just unleashed power's injustices.

That one life is worth as much as any other.

That the Palestinian people (with a population eight times Alaska's, four or five times other U.S. states'), cornered in an unlivable area, have the same rights as any other people on this planet.

That Palestinians - men, women and children crushed by indiscriminate bombs - are not "two-legged animals" as Prime Minister Netanyahu claims (dogs would be treated better). Nor are Israelis "the people of light" fighting "the people of darkness."

That Palestinians aren't terrorists by birth, but one of the peoples most subjected to dehumanization and constant siege, theft, humiliation and unpunished murder for nearly a century.

Yet those daring to protest this historic massacre - one of many - are, what a coincidence, accused of supporting terrorism. Nothing new. State terrorists worldwide have always operated this way, throughout history under all colored flags.

PALESTINE: THE HISTORICAL (AND STRATEGIC) DEHUMANIZATION OF A PEOPLE[1]

ON DECEMBER 4, 1832, President Andrew Jackson, known (where known well) by the nickname Indian Killer, gave a fine speech to his country's Congress. *"Without doubt,"* he said, *"the Republic's interest is having new lands occupied as soon as possible. A country's wealth and strength lies in its population, and the best part are farmers. Independent farmers are everywhere society's foundation and liberty's true friends... The Indians were completely defeated and the band of malcontents expelled or destroyed... Though we had to act harshly, it was necessary; they attacked us unprovoked, and we hope they've learned this salutary lesson forever."*

"They attacked us unprovoked," "we were struck first," "we had to defend ourselves..." These phrases will echo through coming centuries, mobilizing millions upon millions of patriots with extreme fanaticism.

---

[1] May 2021

A century and a half later, in May 1971, the most famous actor and producer of *westerns*, white supremacist propagandist and gun enthusiast John Wayne told *People* magazine that Indian reservations were a socialist vice. No one's responsible for the past, he said, when *"many people needed land and Indians selfishly wanted to keep it."*

These were not scattered tribes but organized nations, as populous as the settlers who defended their own borders while relentlessly pushing others' boundaries—both actions carried out with patriotic pride and fanaticism. The lives of "inferior races" never mattered, nor did the numerous treaties signed with those who possessed lands more coveted than their women. The land of laws violated every law, even its own when stripping neighbors of material possessions. All was done in the name of Liberty, Democracy, God, and some far-fetched biblical interpretation like the myth of Manifest Destiny.

Neither can Native Americans use the Bible to claim ancestral lands held for centuries, nor can Black Americans demand reparations for building a nation whose structures perpetuated ghettos, discrimination, and racial privilege to this day. Nor can Latin Americans reclaim the hundreds of tons of gold and thousands of tons of silver that enriched Europe—still hoarded in central banks to stabilize "civilized" development. This ignores details like guano profits or the colonial legacy entrenched in Latin America's societal structures, culture, and subjugated mentality.

The Israeli-Palestinian conflict is scarcely different, for human nature remains unchanged. So too the strategy of conflating Judaism and the long-suffering Jewish people with the State of Israel and its formidable propaganda machine—more impressive even than its multibillion-dollar military, bankrolled by Washington's billions of dollars annually. Many fall for this flag-waving trap, betraying millennia of resisting—and suffering under—ruling powers. They forget, for instance, that one of European Jewry's longest, most prosperous eras owed to Muslim protection in Spain for nearly eight centuries, until their expulsion and persecution when Arab patrons fell to Christians in 1492. Islam tolerated Jews despite their rejection of Jesus (sacred to Islam) as a true prophet. Christian fanatics did not. They tolerated neither: one group for believing in Muhammad, the other for disbelieving in Jesus.

Not all are deceived. My countless Jewish friends, for example, are too cultured and intelligent to swallow this ploy—as are Jewish communities across Europe and the U.S. brave enough to reject Middle

Eastern apartheid, chanting "not in our name." In Latin America, the attitude is different, perhaps for the same reasons that lead its ruling class to polish monuments without reading their names. Nationalistic confusions are strategic and always serve, like the patriotism of colonizers, those in power.

In the most recent conflict in Cananea (a skirmish, compared to the endless list of tragedies accumulated since the 20th century), in just a couple of days there are already 30 Palestinians and three Israelis dead. As usual, a third of the dead Palestinians are children, but they say they were terrorists. Presidents like Uruguay's Lacalle Pou didn't hesitate. Slow on almost everything, they wasted no time in showing solidarity with only one side of the conflict. The side of security. One doesn't need to know it's not the side that has piled up more dead, because that's a tradition in Gaza, the world's largest ghetto, and a tradition of many Christians that would shame the very teacher they claim to follow: being harsh with those below and soft with those above. It's so pitiful to live defending the strongest, it's downright embarrassing.

The logic is clear: the right to self-defense only applies to some peoples; not to all.

The right to have a country, with its own laws and independent institutions, only applies to one people.

The solidarity of the powerful and their stewards only applies to one people.

As if that weren't enough, the same old formula is applied: the history of attacks and reactions is cut at the most convenient point, and provocation, harassment, and oppression are called defense.

Of course, every life lost is to be mourned. On both sides. But precisely because of that, gentlemen. Precisely because of that, Mr. Presidents, some of us want to know: do Palestinian children, men and women not exist? Do only ordinary men and women show solidarity with them? Is it so hard to have a shred of human dignity and forget about flags and about those who still kill in God's name and for more material reasons?

No, of course, Palestinians never existed. They have the dual status of being invariably terrorists and having never existed at all. A true ontological feat.

Gentlemen in the vain and shameful power of the day: I won't ask what you're afraid of because it's all too obvious. It's also obvious you don't care when choosing the side of power and security, but know that history will be merciless.

If you couldn't care less about history, but the Bible weighs on you, just imagine for a moment that Jesus might have saved himself from becoming another rebel executed by the empire of the day. He only had to show solidarity with Pontius Pilate, with the Pharisees, with the teachers of the law, and with His Excellency Emperor and General Tiberius.

HEBA ABU NADA WAS MURDERED TODAY

ONE OF GAZA'S MOST TALENTED feminist poets and novelists, Heba Abu Nada, was the author of the novel "Oxygen Is Not for the Dead." Yesterday, October 21st, she wrote: "If we die, know that we are satisfied and steadfast, and tell the world, in our name, that we are just people/on the side of truth." Her last poem, written yesterday before being murdered amid Israel's genocide against Palestine, says:

The night in the city is dark
except for the glow of missiles
silent,
except for the sound of bombing
terrifying,
except for the comforting promise of prayer
black,
except for the light of the martyrs.
Good night.

GOOGLE, YOUTUBE, AND MORALFARE[2]

IN MARCH 2022, ONE MONTH AFTER the start of the war in Ukraine, the giant Google, owner of YouTube, warned content producers (though with cosmetic rights, they are the platform's primary workers—those who reach at least 1,000 subscribers and 4,000 viewing hours receive their first dollar) to be cautious with their audiovisual content and refrain from expressing any idea or opinion that "*exploits, dismisses, or condones*" the war in Ukraine.

Naturally, none of these warnings were ever enforced for NATO-led wars, not even the most recent ones in the Middle East and North Africa. On the contrary, the brutal invasion of Iraq based on "false information" and childlike narratives—which left a million dead, millions displaced, and half a continent plunged into the most violent chaos imaginable—was supported by these same media outlets under, for example, the "*Patriot Act*" passed in Washington in October 2001, which did not even allow the publication

---

[2] October 2022

of photos of one's own dead returning home or the foreign dead sinking into oblivion. Moreover, every report "from the scene" had to be accompanied by repeated references to the attack on the Twin Towers. Not to mention more recent wars, massacres, systematic drone bombings, killings hidden from public opinion, inoculated or hijacked rebellions, magni-cides of dictators or rebel leaders like Muammar Gaddafi, and ongoing human rights violations by powerful governments, such as the abuses and mass exterminations of peoples in Yemen, Syria, and Palestine.

A subtle and highly effective form of censorship for small and large producers of cultural, entertainment, or news content on YouTube consisted of the best censorship strategy any democratic or dictatorial system has known in recent centuries—from Jeremy Bentham's Panopticon in the 18th century to the fear among users that the CIA, NSA, or other secret agencies are monitoring their online activities, passing through countless dictatorships, like the military-capitalist dictatorships in Latin America during the 20th century.

In this case, self-censorship began with Google and YouTube's threat of *demonetization*. In other words, you are free to think whatever you want, but if you say something we disagree with, we will stop paying you for your work, and no union can defend you. In fact, this is what happened to many independent journalists on the platform, some of whom are my friends.

In other words, the mega-platforms, born and legally based in the U.S., do not even respect their own country's constitution, which, in its First Amendment, guarantees freedom of expression—whether it's the expression of the KKK, Nazis, Neo-Nazis, or Re-Nazis. This results in a grave contradiction to the extraterritorial application of the same U.S. laws that are enforced even in countries like China, in the facilities of companies like Apple or Microsoft, as if they had diplomatic immunity.

Google capped its threat with the following moral sermon, typical of the double standards of great powers and corporations: the company's policies are violated when, for example, publishing "*dangerous or derogatory content… that incites violen-ce or denies tragic events*" in Ukraine. If there is such a thing as *lawfare*, it's clear that the usual powers have invented *moralfare* (especially in private companies that write their own laws) to hijack principles dear to those below.

Victims are victims in any case (from the Sahara to Madrid, from Libya to Paris, from South Africa and

Congo to London and Brussels, from Guatemala and Chile to Washington, from Syria and Palestine to Ukraine), but *moralfare* is used only to pity and support some victims with the full force of media, propaganda, and international narratives while rendering others invisible.

The mafia of First World corporations is an octopus with global tentacles, and they all share a common factor: *money, media, and power*. Russia's team was excluded from the 2022 Qatar World Cup, without anyone being horrified by the 7,000 migrant deaths preparing the global football festival in that Persian Gulf petro-dictatorship, where—as in Saudi Arabia—there is no room for outrage over oppressed women or NATO women's indignation for media and strategic reasons. FIFA itself was complicit with Italian fascism, which enabled the hosting of football championships in 1934 and 1938; the same was true in Argentina 1978, when the brutal dictatorship of General Videla was not punished but rewarded by the international mafia. The U.S. participated in the 2002 World Cup in South Korea and Japan despite massive bombings, torture, and massacres in Iraq.

In 2011, Sevilla footballer Frederic Kanouté was sanctioned for showing his support for the Palestinian people. As soon as the war in Ukraine began, all broadcasts of matches in the popular and powerful Spanish La Liga were relentlessly accompanied by that country's flag next to the timer, as a show of solidarity against the aggression of a stronger country (the media reports a war of *Russia against Ukraine*, not the more obvious war of *Russia against NATO*).European football clubs, like Atlético de Madrid, illuminated their stadiums with the colors of the Ukrainian flag, for which they received congratulations for their act of heroism and solidarity with Human Rights. The same occurred in other stadiums, like England's Wembley. In many matches of the also powerful English Premier League, players were forced to enter the field carrying the Ukrainian flag, as a sign of sporting neutrality.

As established and practiced by the father of modern propaganda, Edward Bernays, the best way to manage a democracy is by telling citizens what they should think. "*The conscious and intelligent manipulation of the organized habits and opinions of the masses is an important element in democratic society.*" According to a 2022 report by the American Civil Liberties Union (ACLU), "*the U.S. Supreme Court recognized in 1936 that 'an informed public is the most potent of all restraints upon misgovernment.' Yet today, much of our government's business is conducted in secret. There is a sprawling secret apparatus of secret agencies, secret congressional com-mittees, secret courts, and even secret laws. This ever-ex-panding secret state poses a serious threat to individual liberty and undermines the very notion of government of, by, and for the people."*

BY DIVINE RIGHT[3]

IN EARLY MARCH 2010, during U.S. Vice President Joe Biden's visit to Israel, the Israeli government announced new construction plans in the occupied Palestinian territories of East Jerusalem.

The announcement, which was neither the first nor the last, provoked a reaction from the United States. On March 13, Secretary of State Hillary Clinton called the expansionist announcement an insult.

In response, Hagai Ben-Artzi, Prime Minister Benjamin Netanyahu's brother-in-law, reacted defensively, declaring on army radio that the American president was "antisemitic, anti-Israeli, and anti-Jewish" and urged his brother-in-law to say "no" to American interference. Above all, the meddling of Dr. Obama, who "not only dislikes the prime minister but also dislikes the people of Israel."

Prime Minister Netanyahu corrected his brother-in-law's remarks in an official statement: "I am deeply grateful for President Obama's commitment to Israel's security, which he has expressed many times."

---

[3] March 2010

However, Ben-Artzi was forced to do the same, albeit unofficially, stating that he does "know his brother-in-law the prime minister's opinions about Obama" but cannot disclose what is said "in private conversations."

Days after what news agencies called the worst crisis in decades between the U.S. and Israel, the Israeli prime minister traveled to America to meet with President Obama. During this off-the-record meeting with no cameras or unofficial recordings, news of a new construction plan in another disputed area of Jerusalem surprised both the American president and the Israeli minister.

The president was angered by the news of the plan, and the minister was angered by the news itself. He accused the Israeli left of leaking it and failing to prioritize Israel's interests above all else.

Shortly afterward, on March 22, in a speech before one of the world's most powerful lobbies, the American Israel Public Affairs Committee (AIPAC), Prime Minister Netanyahu was very clear: "Peace cannot be imposed from the outside. It can only come through direct negotiations in which we develop an environment of mutual trust" ("Peace cannot be imposed from the outside. It can only come through direct negotiations in which we develop mutual trust.")

Which demonstrates that the Palestinian issue is an internal Israeli matter.

According to the authors of *The Israel Lobby and U.S. Foreign Policy* (2007), professors John Mearsheimer (University of Chicago) and Stephen Walt (Harvard University), the American Israel Public Affairs Committee is one of the most powerful lobbies in Washington. "The lobby does not want an open debate because it might lead Americans to question the level of support they offer [to the Israeli government]. Consequently, pro-Israel organizations work hard to influence institutions that shape public opinion [...]. The lobby's greatest difficulty has been in trying to suppress debate on university campuses [...] What is most concerning are the efforts by Jewish groups to pressure Congress into establishing monitoring mechanisms over professors' statements."

John Mearsheimer and Stephen Walt conclude that "no discussion of this lobby would be complete without analyzing one of its primary weapons: the accusation of antisemitism."

Of course, it's possible this study was written under the influence of antisemitism.

The Israeli government exercises its legitimate right to self-defense, especially against those Palestinians who in their speeches deny Israel's existence. One mechanism of this self-defense involves accepting Palestine's existence in speeches while denying it in practice.

Undoubtedly, Israel will one day allow the Palestinian people to have their own country, their own state, their own laws. But perhaps that will happen when the State of Israel no longer feels threatened.

In his American speech, Prime Minister Netanyahu stated that "just as the Palestinians expect Israel to recognize a Palestinian state, we expect the Palestinians to recognize the Jewish state" ("*just as the Palestinians expect Israel to recognize a Palestinian state, we expect the Palestinians to recognize the Jewish state.*")

All of which demonstrates that the proper use of language is more important than any practical impropriety, such as colonization by force to create an atmosphere of trust, or the suspension of human rights for peoples hostile to the good intentions of prime ministers.

It is also possible that these latter points are arguments made by violent fanatics, by Palestinian youths throwing stones, by terrorist widows planting bombs, by armed militias firing rockets at Israeli farmers—threatening the existence of the Israeli state—and who, since January 2009, have already killed one Thai farmer.

And what is worse and less convenient than stones—perhaps these are the arguments of intellectuals, many of them Jewish, who are influenced by bad ideologies and occasionally dare to criticize the actions of the Israeli government, which is the expression of its people's opinion in the first instance and of God's will in the last.

The only truth is that, as Prime Minister Benjamin Netanyahu has said, the Jewish people built Jerusalem three thousand years ago. Any archaeological evidence suggesting an earlier settlement is disregarded, not only because it does not come from sacred scripture but also because the scientific account refers not to a holy city but to a Canaanite settlement.

Some changes have been made since then, as in Mexico City after God delivered Tenochtitlán to Hernán Cortés and Catholicism.

Some temples no longer exist in Jerusalem. Others have been built in their place or on top of them. Some housing has been added, some towers, some streets paved, some traffic lights installed. In short, some adjustments have been made over the last two thousand years while Palestine and Jerusalem were illegally held by Persians, Greeks, Romans, and Arabs.

Of course, these latter peoples don't count. What matters is who was there first. Except for those unfaithful Canaanites who inhabited Palestine before the people of Moses arrived and took possession by divine mandate.

In his speech before the Israeli Committee, Prime Minister Netanyahu stated: "*My first name is Benjamin. This name is a thousand years old. Benjamin was the name of Jacob's son. One of Benjamin's brothers was named Shimon, which happens to be the same name as my good friend, Shimon Peres, the President of Israel. Approximately four thousand years ago, Benjamin, Simon, and their ten brothers roamed those hills of Jerusalem. The Jewish people built Jerusalem three thousand years ago and are now building it again*".

All of which may well align with the Old Testament:

"*Then the Lord said to Moses, 'Do not fear him, for I have delivered him into your hand, with all his people and his land; and you shall do to him as you did to Sihon king of the Amorites, who dwelt in Heshbon.' So they defeated him, his sons, and all his people, until there was no survivor left, and they took possession of his land*". (Numbers 21:34-35)

Then came America.

THE SLOW SUICIDE OF THE WEST[4]

*"The struggle is not—nor should it be—between Eastern-
ers and Westerners; the struggle is between intolerance and
imposition, between diversity and homogenization, between respect for the other and their contempt or annihilation. What is at stake today is not just protecting the West
against terrorists, from here and there, but—above all—it
is crucial to protect it from itself. Simply replicating any of
its monstrous inventions would be enough to lose everything achieved thus far in terms of respect for Human
Rights. Starting with respect for diversity. And it is highly
likely that this will happen within ten years if we do not
react in time."* (2002)

SOME CELEBRITIES from the 20th century, demonstrating an irreversible senile decline, have devoted themselves to spreading the famous ideology of the "clash
of civilizations"—which was already vulgar in itself—
beginning their reasoning with conclusions, in the
best tradition of classical theology. Such as the a pri-
ori, 19th-century assertion that *"Western culture is*

---

[4] Montevideo, January 8, 2002

superior to all others," and, as if that weren't enough, it is a moral duty to repeat it.

From this Western Superiority, the famously brilliant Italian journalist Oriana Fallaci recently penned such gems as: "If in some countries women are so stupid as to accept the chador or even the veil with a grid over their eyes, too bad for them. (...) And if their husbands are so foolish as to abstain from wine or beer, likewise." Wow, what intellectual rigor. "How disgusting!"—she continued writing, first in the *Corriere della Sera* and later in her bestseller "The Rage and the Pride," referring to Africans who had urinated in an Italian square—"These sons of Allah sure have long piss streams! A race of hypocrites." "Even if they were completely innocent, even if none among them wanted to destroy the Leaning Tower of Pisa or Giotto's Tower, none wanted to force me to wear the chador, none wanted to burn me at the stake of a new Inquisition, their presence alarms me. It unsettles me." In short: even if those Black people were completely innocent, their presence unsettles her just the same. For Fallaci, this is not racism but "cold, lucid, and rational rage." And, as if that weren't enough, a brilliant observation about immigrants in general: "Besides, there's another thing I don't understand. If they really are so poor, who gives them the money for plane or boat tickets to Italy? Couldn't Osama bin Laden be paying for at least part of it?" ...Poor Galileo, poor Camus, poor Simone de Beauvoir, poor Michel Foucault.

Incidentally, let us remember that, though this woman writes without understanding—as she herself admitted—these words made it into a book that has sold half a million copies, one that lacks neither reasoning nor clichés, such as "I am an atheist, thank God."Nor historical curiosities of this sort: "How does that square with polygamy and the principle that women shouldn't be photographed? Because this too is in the Quran," implying that seventh-century Arabs were quite advanced in optics. Nor her repeated doses of humor, like these weighty arguments: "And let's face it: our cathedrals are more beautiful than mosques and synagogues, aren't they? They're more beautiful than Protestant churches too." As Atilio says, she's got the sparkle of Brigitte Bardot. As if we needed to get tangled in debates about whether the Leaning Tower of Pisa is more beautiful than the Taj Mahal. And again with European tolerance: "I'm telling you precisely because it's been clearly defined for centuries that our cultural identity cannot withstand a migratory wave composed of people who, one way or another, want to change our way of life. Our values. I'm telling you there's no place among us for muezzins, for minarets, for fake teetotalers, for their damned medieval ways, for their damned chadors. And if there were room, I wouldn't give it to them." She concludes with a warning to her editor: "I warn you: don't ever ask me for anything again. Least of all to participate in vain polemics. I've said what I had to say. Rage and pride commanded me." This was already clear from the start and, incidentally, denies one of democracy's foundational principles—and tolerance since ancient Greece: debate and the right to reply—the competition of arguments over insults.

But since I don't possess a name as famous as Fallaci's—justly earned, we've no reason to doubt—I can't content myself with insults. Being native to an underdeveloped country and not even famous like Maradona, I've no choice but to resort to the old custom of using arguments.

Let's examine this. The very phrase "Western culture" is as ambiguous as "Eastern culture" or "Islamic culture," because each consists of a diverse and often contradictory collection of other "cultures." Just consider that "Western culture" encompasses not only countries as different as Cuba and the United States, but irreconcilable historical periods within the same geographic region—tiny Europe or even smaller

Germany, where both Goethe and Adolf Hitler walked, Bach and the *skinheads*. Moreover, let's not forget that Hitler and the Ku Klux Klan (in the name of Christ and the White Race), Stalin (in the name of Reason and atheism), Pinochet (in the name of Democracy and Liberty), and Mussolini (in his own name) were all recent, representative products of self-proclaimed "Western culture." What could be more Western than democracy and concentration camps? What could be more Western than the Declaration of Human Rights and the bloody, degenerate dictatorships in Spain and Latin America that pushed the limits of imagination? What could be more Western than Christianity, which both healed and saved while also murdering through the Holy Inquisition? What could be more Western than modern military academies or the ancient monasteries where, under Pope Innocent IV's initiative and based on Roman Law, the art of torture was taught with refined sadism? Or did Marco Polo import all that from the Middle East? What could be more Western than the atomic bomb and the millions dead or disappeared under fascist, communist, and even "democratic" regimes? What could be more Western than military invasions and the suppression of entire peoples under so-called "preemptive bombings"?

All this is the dark side of the West, and nothing guarantees we're safe from any of it simply because we can't get along with our neighbors—who have been there for over 1,400 years—with the only difference being that the world is now globalized (globalized by the West) and they possess the primary energy source driving the world economy (for now), along with the same hatred and resentment as Oriana Fallaci. Let's not forget that the Spanish Inquisition, more state-run than others, arose from hostility toward Moors and Jews and didn't end with Spain's "Progress and Salvation" but with the burning of thousands of human beings.

Yet the West also represents Democracy, Freedom, Human Rights, and the struggle for women's rights—at least the attempt to achieve them, and the farthest humanity has gotten so far. And what has always been the foundation of these four pillars if not tolerance?

Fallaci wants us to believe that "Western culture" is a pure, singular product, untouched by others. But if anything defines the West, it has been precisely the opposite: we are the result of countless cultures, starting with Hebrew culture (not to mention Amenhotep IV) and continuing through nearly all others—the Chaldeans, the Greeks, the Chinese, the Hindus, the

Africans of the south and north, and the rest of the cultures now uniformly labeled "Islamic." Not long ago, it wouldn't have been necessary to remind anyone that when, across all of Europe, the Christian Church persecuted, tortured, and burned alive those who disagreed with ecclesiastical authorities or committed the sin of engaging in research (or simply because they were lone women—i.e., witches)—all in the name of Love—the Islamic world was spreading arts and sciences, not only their own but also those of the Chinese, Hindus, Jews, and Greeks. And this doesn't mean butterflies fluttered and violins played everywhere: the geographical distance between Baghdad and Córdoba was, at the time, almost astronomical.

But Oriana Fallaci not only denies the diverse and contradictory composition of any of the cultures in question—she outright refuses to recognize the Eastern part as a culture at all. "It annoys me to even speak of two cultures," she wrote. Then she delivers an astonishing display of historical ignorance: "To place them on the same level, as if they were two parallel realities, of equal weight and measure. Because behind our civilization stand Homer, Socrates, Plato, Aristotle, and Phidias, among many others. There is ancient Greece with its Parthenon and its discovery of

Democracy. There is ancient Rome with its grandeur, its laws, and its conception of Law. With its sculpture, literature, and architecture. Its palaces and amphitheaters, its aqueducts, bridges, and roads."

Does Fallaci need reminding that between all that and us stands the ancient Islamic Empire, without which everything would have burned—I speak of books and people, not the Colosseum—thanks to centuries of well-European, well-Western ecclesiastical terrorism? As for the grandeur of Rome and its "conception of Law," we'll discuss that another day, because here there's clear black and white to recall. And let's set aside Islamic literature and architecture, which have nothing to envy in Fallaci's Rome, as any moderately educated person knows.

Now, lastly: "And finally," wrote Fallaci, "there is science. A science that has discovered many diseases and cures them. I am still alive, for now, thanks to our science, not Muhammad's. A science that has changed the face of this planet with electricity, the radio, the telephone, television... So then, let's ask the fatal question: and behind the other culture, what is there?"

Fatal answer: behind our science stand the Egyptians, the Chaldeans, the Indians, the Greeks, the Chinese, the Arabs, the Jews, and the Africans. Or does Fallaci believe everything arose spontaneously in the last fifty years? This lady ought to be reminded that Pythagoras took his philosophy from Egypt and Chaldea (Iraq)—including his famous mathematical formula, which we use not only in architecture but also in proving Einstein's Special Theory of Relativity—just as another sage and mathematician named Thales of Miletus did. Both traveled through the Middle East with minds far more open than Fallaci's when she did. The hypothetical-deductive method—the foundation of scientific epistemology—originated among Egyptian priests (start with Klimovsky, please); the zero and square roots, as well as countless mathematical and astronomical discoveries we now teach in schools, were born in India and Iraq; the alphabet was invented by the Phoenicians (ancient Lebanese) and likely the first form of globalization the world ever knew. Zero was not an Arab invention but an Indian one, though it was the Arabs who brought it to the West. To make matters worse, the advanced Roman Empire not only had no concept of zero—without which modern mathematics and space travel would be unimaginable—but also used a cumbersome counting and calculation system that persisted until the late Middle Ages. Even at the dawn of the Renaissance, there were still businessmen using Roman numerals, refusing to switch to Arabic numerals due to racial and religious prejudices, leading to all sorts of miscalculations and legal disputes. On another note, let's not even mention that the birth of the Modern Era stemmed from European culture's contact—after centuries of religious repression—first with Islamic culture and later with Greek culture. Or did anyone think scholastic rationality was a consequence of the tortures practiced in holy dungeons? In the early 12th century, the Englishman Adelard of Bath embarked on an extensive study tour through southern Europe, Syria, and Palestine. Upon his return, Adelard introduced to underdeveloped England a paradigm still upheld by famous scientists like Stephen Hawking: God had created Nature in such a way that it could be studied and explained without His intervention (Here lies the other pillar of science, historically denied by the Roman Church). Adelard even reproached the thinkers of his time for being dazzled by the prestige of authorities— starting with the Greek Aristotle, of course. For this, he coined the motto "reason against authority" and called himself "modernus." "I have learned from my Arab teachers to take reason as my guide," he wrote, "but you are ruled only by what authority says." A compatriot of Fallaci's, Gerard of Cremona, introduced Europe to the writings of the "Iraqi" astronomer and mathematician Al-Khwarizmi, inventor of algebra, algorithms, and Arabic decimal calculus; he translated Ptolemy from Arabic—since even the astronomical theory of an official Greek like him wasn't found in Christian Europe—along with dozens of medical treatises, such as those of Ibn Sina and the Iranian al-Razi, author of the first scientific treatise on smallpox and measles, for which today he would likely face persecution.*modernus.* "I have learned from my Arab teachers to take reason as my guide," he wrote, "but you are ruled only by what authority says." A compatriot of Fallaci's, Gerard of Cremona, introduced Europe to the writings of the "Iraqi" astronomer and mathematician Al-Khwarizmi, inventor of algebra, algorithms, and Arabic decimal calculus; he translated Ptolemy from Arabic—since even the astronomical theory of an official Greek like him wasn't found in Christian Europe—along with dozens of medical treatises, such as those of Ibn Sina and the Iranian al-Razi, author of the first scientific treatise on smallpox and measles, for which today he would likely face persecution.

We could go on listing examples like these, which the Italian journalist ignores, but we've already covered them in a book, and that's not what matters most now.

What's at stake today isn't just protecting the West from terrorists, here and there, but—perhaps above all—it's crucial to protect it from itself. Replicating any of its monstrous inventions would be enough to undo all the progress made so far in respecting Human Rights. Starting with respect for diversity. And it's highly likely this will happen in ten years if we don't react in time.

The seed is already there, and all it needs is a little water. I've heard the following phrase dozens of times: "The only good thing Hitler did was kill all those Jews." No more, no less. And I haven't heard it from any Muslim—perhaps because I live in a country where they barely exist—nor even from descendants of Arabs. I've heard it from neutral locals or descendants of Europeans. In every case, I've silenced my interlocutor by reasoning: "What's your last name? Gutiérrez, Pauletti, Wilson, Marceau... So, sir, you're not German, much less of pure Aryan blood. Which means long before Hitler finished with the Jews, he'd have started by killing your grandparents and anyone with a profile or skin color like yours." We're now facing the same risk: if we start persecuting Arabs or Muslims, we'll not only prove we've learned nothing, but soon we'll end up persecuting their kin: Bedouins, North Africans, Roma, southern Spaniards, Sephardic

Jews, Latin American Jews, Central Americans, south-ern Mexicans, northern Mormons, Hawaiians, Chi-nese, Indians, and so on.

Not long ago, another Italian, Umberto Eco, summed up a wise warning: "We are a plural civiliza-tion because we allow mosques to be built in our countries, and we cannot renounce this just because in Kabul they jail Christian missionaries (...) We be-lieve our culture is mature because it knows how to tolerate diversity, and the barbarians are those within our culture who do not."

As Freud and Jung said, what no one would ever wish to commit becomes the object of prohibition; and as Baudrillard noted, rights are established pre-cisely when they've been lost. Islamic terrorists have achieved what they wanted, doubly so. The West sud-denly appears stripped of its finest virtues, built cen-tury upon century, now preoccupied with reproducing its own flaws and copying the flaws of others—such as authoritarianism and the preventive persecution of innocents. So much time spent impos-ing its culture on other regions of the planet, only to now allow itself to be imposed upon by a morality that, at its best, was never its own. Virtues like toler-ance and self-criticism were never part of its weakness, as some claim, but quite the opposite: they made possible some form of progress, both ethical and material. Democracy and Science never developed from narcissistic worship of one's own culture but from critical opposition to it. And until recently, this wasn't just the work of "cursed intellectuals" but many social resistance groups—like the bourgeoisie in the 18th century, unions in the 20th, and investigative journalism until yesterday, now replaced by propaganda in these miserable times of ours. Even the swift erosion of privacy is another symptom of this moral colonization. Only now, instead of religious control, we'll be policed by Military Security. The Big Brother who sees and hears all will eventually impose masks on us like those we see in the East, with the sole purpose of ensuring we're unrecognizable when walking down the street or making love.

The struggle is not—nor should it be—between Easterners and Westerners; the struggle is between intolerance and imposition, between diversity and homogenization, between respect for the other and their contempt or annihilation. Writings like Oriana Fallaci's "The Rage and the Pride" are not a defense of Western culture but a treacherous attack, an insulting pamphlet against the best of the West. The proof is that simply swapping the word "East" for "West," along with a few geographic references, would reveal the text as Taliban fanaticism. Those of us who feel neither Rage nor Pride for any race or culture instead feel nostalgia for bygone days—which were never good, but never this bad either.

Years ago, I was in the United States and saw a beautiful mural in the United Nations building in New York (if I recall correctly), depicting men and women of different races and religions—I believe the composition was based on a somewhat arbitrary pyramid, but that's beside the point. Below, in golden letters, was a commandment taught by Confucius in China and repeated for millennia across the East until it became a Western principle: "Do unto others as you would have them do unto you." In English, it sounds musical, and even those who don't speak the language sense it speaks to reciprocity between oneself and others. I don't understand why we should erase this commandment from our walls—the foundation of any democracy and rule of law, the bedrock of the West's finest dreams—just because others have suddenly forgotten it. Or replaced it with an ancient biblical principle that Christ himself abolished: "an eye for an eye, a tooth for a tooth." Today, this translates into an inversion of Confucius's maxim, becoming something like: do unto others everything they have done to you—the familiar never-ending story.

WHEN THE TRUTH OF WAR SEEPS INTO OUR WORLD OF ILLUSIONS[5]

UMBERTO ECO, SOMEWHERE IN the pages of *La definizione dell'arte* (1968), wrote that any ordinary object found on the street gains new meaning when placed in a museum. Its artistic and semiotic value lies in decontextualization. The Russian formalists had grasped something similar when, in the early 20th century, they analyzed the importance of (how to put it?) *agrammaticality* in poetry—how an unexpected, unusual word captures the reader's attention. In this way, a gear, a noun, could take on new meaning, more potent, more autonomous (Latin American modernists had already experimented with this in the 19th century).

This semiotic dynamic plays out in digital globalization, where the cold indifference of phenomena collides with the unbearable tragedy of moral suffering.

The recent video showing the tearless, stunned reaction of a child victim of aerial bomb-ings in Aleppo,

---

[5] August 2016

Syria, became what is so dubiously called "viral." Every so often, the world is shaken by these faces of innocent victims. A similar case was that of Aylan Kurdi, another Syrian child drowned in his parents' attempt to reach Europe's shores.

Both tragedies obviously share many elements. But so do their media-driven reactions. Whether the child dead on a Turkish beach or the one in Aleppo, the common thread that made them "viral" was de-contextualization—not the revelation of any truth about ongoing wars or the long-standing abuses of power.

Since the invasion of Iraq and long before (Vietnam, Lebanon, Guatemala, Palestine, Western Sahara, Sierra Leone, Nigeria... to name just a few, the most forgotten in recent years), we've seen children covered in dust, dismembered, massacred in outrageous numbers. None of those images provoked the mass reactions seen in the two recent cases.

Why?

Well, I don't think it takes a genius to realize the explanation is psychological rather than purely moral. In both cases, the children's dramas—distant to the West and to the wealthy East and Middle East—were transposed onto a familiar context, one belonging to developed countries or at least those not at war. The beach in Kos was a European beach, far from conflict; the Turkish officer who retrieved the body wearing latex gloves could have been someone we know from our own Western beaches.

Even more evident is the recent case of Omran in Aleppo.

The first remarkable element is Omran's absence of crying, the realization of being hurt when touching his face and seeing his bloodied hand. The painfully humble gesture of that innocent little boy who, almost as if he shouldn't, wipes the blood from his hand on the immaculate orange chair and timidly looks around. His expression signifies, even if due to shock or confusion, everything we wouldn't expect from a five-year-old child: the absence of tears amid a tragedy our children have never experienced. Our children know how to cry, and in a consumerist world they practically cry about everything. Omran can't even afford the luxury of tears.

But let's examine a less obvious element, though it's the first thing we see: the image's composition. The boy blurred by debris wounds and dust from the airstrike (whose objective was to protect him; we won't question the good intentions of world powers) is seated in an immaculate orange chair, next to other impeccably orange equipment from the rescuers.

This alone creates a brutal visual contrast. But even more striking is the symbolic contrast: fragility, innocence, transposed into our world, the modern world - immaculate, functional, civilized.

Through symbolic transference, the child becomes one of our neighbors or one of our own relatives living through a tragedy we can't contemplate without being moved, without feeling compelled to contribute something to alleviate that tragedy, almost like someone offering an aspirin to a cancer patient. Perhaps this is the most positive aspect of all the sensitivity shown by those who don't live in war zones.

And yet, almost invariably, after the catharsis that shows how good we are, most people are always ready to forget or sink into inaction.

Some might say the judgment that "most people are always ready to forget" is unfair or arbitrary. True, it's very difficult to quantify this group; I wouldn't even presume to exclude myself. However, judging by the endless tradition of wars and counter-wars, invasions and interventions that normally precede civil wars and the terrorist groups that consequently flourish and multiply - later justifying new interventions and more bombs - it would seem that power indeed always counts on a majority of indifferent people who occasionally get moved to tears when discovering the consequences of their poor choices, for which they never accept any responsibility.

HUMAN LIFE AS COLLATERAL DAMAGE[6]

Our dead are real because they hurt

A FEW DAYS AGO A CHILD DIED of hunger and another of diarrhea.Shortly after, worms ate a thirteen-month-old baby alive. There's no need for graphic details. It's enough to acknowledge it and not dismiss it as some climatic phenomenon but as genuine social injustice.

But these dead children are children from the margins. Forgotten. They're collateral damage. They don't hurt.

Every time a child dies of hunger, the State loses its reason for existence. On this point, we must say the State has repeatedly lost its mind. If society's greatest Institution can fix a traffic light every time it breaks down, how is it incapable of preventing a child from starving to death? I've often heard that a large percentage of human beings who sleep on the streets, their heads resting on sidewalks at zero degrees Celsius, enduring both nature's violence and the moral violence

---

[6] June 2003

of being seen in such degradation, refuse to go to shelters where they'd have food and beds. Hence these individuals are responsible for their wretched condition. In English it even sounds refined: they're *homeless*. But how many of us wouldn't go insane under similarly violent and repeated circumstances like these people endure?

But since the poor are *responsible* for their poverty, just as alcoholics and drug addicts are responsible for their vices, we can leave them abandoned and the world will keep turning. Now, if a man threatens to jump from a tenth floor, what does the State do? In theory, that man has every right to do as he pleases with his existence. Yet no one would dream of letting him exercise that right. Why? We'd always argue that such a person isn't in their right mind and therefore we must help them abandon their attempt. So we send firefighters, police officers and psychologists to *persuade him* against his attempt, lest he dirty the street and set a bad example. Is this right? Beyond philosophical discussions about rights, our intuition screams yes. So why do we leave a man lying in the street? Why doesn't society's greatest organization, the State, take responsibility for every child that starves to death, instead of blaming a mother who lives in a garbage dump and has already stopped thinking?

Wrong—this is the tree with dry leaves. Now let's try to see the forest.

For decades, the Río de la Plata was a river of immigrants. Millions of men and women disembarked ships onto this unknown land to plant their race and customs. Most were Europeans, proud representatives of an advanced culture, of a history full of great empires and ominous dominations, which was often confused with a nonexistent race: the white race. Yet most of those grandparents who stepped off the ships were illiterate, victims of the most obscene persecutions or common criminals. Generally, people without much reason to feel proud. Not because they were poor and illiterate, but because they came from a sick, warlike and puritanical Europe, most often dragging deep prejudices and useless moral rigidities that resembled inhumanity and lies more than wisdom.

A minor incident that occurred in Buenos Aires port perfectly illustrates some of those conquerors—who weren't without virtues but who generally did everything possible to forget their flaws, the very ones anthropology tried to disguise in books. The miracle was recounted to me by my uncle Caíto Albernaz, an uneducated farmer who nonetheless kept books beside his plow and possessed an ethical intelligence too refined to be heard without irritation—a man destroyed many years ago by the military dictatorship. I was still a child when I heard him tell this story with his characteristic brevity, as we listened to the song or perhaps the complaint of a nocturnal bird, its location impossible to pinpoint across the vast horizon at dusk: "Still clutching their suitcases, a group of immigrants crossed paths with another group of a different nationality, likely from some peripheral European country. Then, one said to another: *Our language is superior because it's understandable.*"

Over time, this flash of ignorance became buried beneath a thick layer of culture. Yet deep within our Western hearts, that primitive attitude survives—the belief that our own language is the best language, our morality the finest morality, and (though it pains us to admit) our dead the only true victims. Recognizing this requires no university degree, but rather the sensitivity of that farmer who knew how to listen to birds.

Throughout the 20th century, one ethical principle justified every genocide and massacre, whether large-scale or small: the notion that "the ends justify the means." As expected, those noble ends never materialized, and consequently, the means became perpetual—the means transformed into ends themselves. (This often happens with Causes when they harden into ideologies, or with Faith when it ossifies into dogma.) The logic is doubly flawed, for if one seeks to defend life through death, employing this ultimate recourse makes the intended achievement impossible—unless that achievement happens to be indiscriminate resurrection.

Over time, rhetorics and ideologies have shifted—but only shifted. They've never truly vanished. In fact, the precept that "the ends justify the means" remains as potent today as it was under Stalin or Nero. Now expressed in more technical and less philosophical terms, the same concept goes by the phrase "collateral damage."

Let's examine this more closely. Over the past fifty years, the world's major powers have conducted military interventions to uphold Order, Peace, Freedom, and Democracy. We won't question this premise—doing so would complicate our analysis from the outset. Naturally, each of these life-defending interventions has produced casualties. Unlike wars of old, the dead are rarely soldiers (making theirs one of the world's safest professions—safer than journalism, medicine, or construction work) and never include the architects of these high-stakes ventures. As a general rule, the new dead are always civilians—some elderly person who couldn't run fast enough, some reckless youth with no voice or vote, some pregnant woman, some aborted fetus.

Let us look for a moment at these deaths that neither touch us nor stain us. Are they unforeseen deaths? I think not. No one can be surprised that there are deaths in a military attack. Death and war share historical ties, just as war and corporate interests do. These deaths are so predictable that they have been collectively defined as "collateral damage." It is not true that "smart bombs" are dumb; even a genius makes mistakes—we all know that. Now, the ethical problem arises when we unquestioningly accept that this "collateral damage" is, in any case, inevitable and never stops the action that produces it. Why? Because there are things more important than "collateral damage"—that is, there are things more important than human life. Or at least a certain kind of human life.

And here lies the second ethical problem. Accepting that in a bombing, the deaths of hundreds of innocent men, children, and women can be defined as "collateral damage" is accepting that there exist human lives of "collateral value." Now, if there are human lives of collateral value, why initiate such an action in defense of life? Reason and intuition tell us that this principle carries the implicit, unquestioned idea that there exist human lives of "capital value."

One moment. Faced with such a grotesque conclusion, we must ask ourselves whether we have erred in our reasoning. To do so, we must perform a mental verification exercise. Let us conduct the experiment. Let us ask: What would have happened if, for every five Black or Asian children torn apart by "collateral damage," one or two white children had died—children with full names, a legible address, a past, and a culture shared with the pilots who dropped the bombs? What would have happened if, for every unavoidable instance of "collateral damage," our own neighbors had died? What would have happened if, to "liberate" a distant country, we had to sacrifice a hundred children in our own city as unavoidable "collateral damage"? Would it have been different? But how—how could the death of a distant, unknown, innocent girl with a dirty face be different from the death of a child who lives near us and speaks our language? Which death is more horrible? Which death is more just, and which more unjust? Which of the two innocents deserved to live more?

Surely, nearly everyone would agree that both innocents had the same right to life. Neither more nor less. So why are some innocent deaths "collateral damage," while others could alter any military plan and, above all, any electoral outcome?

While it may seem entirely legitimate for a country to initiate military actions in self-defense against aggression, is it equally legitimate to kill foreign innocents in defense of one's own innocents—even under the logic of "collateral damage"? Is it legitimate to condemn the murder of one's own innocents while simultaneously promoting actions that end the lives of foreign innocents in the name of something better and nobler?

Closer to home—what would happen if worms stopped eating poor children and started eating rich ones? What would happen if, due to administrative negli-gence, children of our heroic and indispensable *well-to-do class* began to die?

An "ethical cleansing" should begin with semantic cleansing: we should strike out the adjective "collateral" and underline the noun "effect." Because the innocents shattered by economic or armed violence are the purest and most direct Effect of the action—just like that, without euphemistic softening. Let it hurt whoever it may. Everything else is debatable.

This blind attitude of the Knowledge Society resembles in every way the proud belief that "our language is better because it's understandable." Only with a tragically heightened intensity, which could be translated as follows: *our dead are real because they hurt.*

HUMAN SHIELDS[7]

LAST MONDAY THE 17TH, AT AN ELEGANT table, President George Bush, believing himself in private, said to Tony Blair—who that day sported an enormous, pristine, very English pink tie—: *"what they need to do is get Syria to get Hezbollah to stop doing this sh..., and it's over."* ("what they have to do is force Syria to make Hezbollah stop this shit, and that's it"). He was referring to the new conflict, bombing, massacre, absurdity between Israel and Lebanon, or between Israel and the Hezbollah guerrilla—this point remains unclear. The English newspaper Daily Mirror, scandalized, headlined: "Bush, start by respecting our minister."

In 1941, Erich Fromm psychoanalyzed (in Fear of Freedom) that gold is equivalent to shit, and a child's retention of it foreshadows the character of capitalism. From the perspective of historical critique, the U.S. president is right about one thing: this is shit. Oh, let's not be so refined: even if the toilets have golden faucets, civilization still stands upon its sewers.

---

[7] July 2006

But let's get to the point. I have always defended Israel's right to defend itself. I have never hesitated to publish an essay, or whatever, pointing out the contradictions and moral sickness of antisemitism. And I will continue to do so because there is one thing I cannot compromise on, one thing where I am intolerant: above any sect, above any arbitrary division, above any mediocre and arrogant fanaticism—racism, sexism, classism—above any ridiculous sentiment of hereditary nobility's superiority, humanity is one, a single race. A race always sick, but the only one we have and to which we cannot cease to belong, even if at times we envy the more straightforward life of dogs.

Despite all this, I could never justify the massacre of even a single innocent person, let alone hundreds, under the argument that terrorists might be hiding among them. This rhetoric has become a broken record, while the victims—what a coincidence—are almost always, overwhelmingly, the innocent, the masses, the anonymous, whether Arab or Jewish, Iraqi or American, Macua or Maconde. Every now and then an enemy leader dies, of course, which serves to justify the success of all this self-inflicted horror.

Someone who plants a bomb and kills ten, a hundred people, is a monster, a terrorist. But killing hundreds of innocents with "smarter" bombs, from afar and above—does that somehow become a triumph of International Law and Progress for Peace? Terrorists are criminals for using human shields; and the other leaders (I don't know what to call them)—are they not equally criminal for bombing those "shields" as if they were stone walls rather than the innocent flesh of a people? Because if we claim that those children, youths, elders, and women aren't even innocent, then we're as sick as the terrorists. With a touch of hypocrisy, of course.

Now, what can we expect from a bombarded people? Love for their neighbor? Understanding? More than that: can we expect even a shred of rationality from someone who has lost their family, torn apart by a bomb—even if it's a bomb loaded with Law, Justice, and Morality? We can't expect this miracle from either side. The difference lies—we assume—in that a terrorist has no interest in any form of rationality or understanding of the other side, whereas we would hope the other side appeals to this human faculty, if not as an ethical value, then at least as a strategy for survival, co-existence, or any of those noble things we always hear in speeches. This absence of rationality in human hatred is a victory for terror. Those who create or fuel it are responsible, regardless of whether the chicken or the egg came first.

To complete our pessimism, every escalation of indiscriminate violence in the world serves as both the clearest warning and the perfect excuse for other misguided souls to understand the message: better a well-armed suspect than an unarmed innocent. Just as certain "democratic" politicians secure blind obedience from their followers through fear of the adversary, so too do the terrorists of the day recruit followers from this sowing of hatred. Hatred is the most democratic poison in which humanity languishes; we suspect it will be impossible to eradicate from our species, but we also know that, despite its postmodern disrepute, only rationality can keep it confined within the hellish recesses of the individual and collective subconscious.

The U.S. president complained that Kofi Annan, the UN Secretary-General, favors an immediate cease-fire. "He thinks that's enough to fix the problem." No, of course not—when has any measure ever been enough to stop the slaughter in this world? But stopping the killing is something, isn't it? Or do you think two hundred dead in a week is just a minor detail? Would it still be a minor detail if half of them spoke English?

In 1896, Ángel Ganivet observed in his book Idearium español, with skepticism and bitterness: "An army that fights with long-range weapons, rapid-fire machine guns, and heavy artillery, even if it leaves the field strewn with corpses, is a glorious army; and if the corpses are of the black race, then it is said there are no such corpses. A soldier who fights hand-to-hand and kills his enemy with a bayonet begins to seem brutal to us; a man in civilian clothes who fights and kills seems like a murderer to us. We don't focus on the act. We focus on the appearance."

My thesis has always been this: it's not true that history never repeats itself—it repeats itself constantly. What doesn't repeat are merely appearances. My initial warning also remains unchanged: indiscriminate violence doesn't just sow death but, worse still—hatred.

POSTSCRIPT 2024

I HOLD AN ILLEGAL OPINION ABOUT ███████████ IN ██████

ON MAY 1ST, 2024, the U.S. House of Representatives passed the *Antisemitism Awareness Act*. The urgency stemmed from massive protests against ████████ across dozens of universities.

From now on, any public or academic discussion about what constitutes antisemitism is permanently defined by law, granting Education Secretary ████████ Miguel Cardona increased power to determine punishments and sanctions at his discretion regarding antisemitism and the correct resolution to the Trolley Problem ethical dilemma. All debates must operate within the framework established by the leader of the Free World, where such definitions "*shall not be subject to interpretation*" (Sec. 6-a).

The new law claims foundation in the 1964 *Civil Rights Act* prohibiting discrimination based on race or national origin—a remarkable ████████, considering that legislation resulted from protests mirroring current movements. Those were intense, courageous demonstrations against racial segregation, white supremacy, imperialism, and the Vietnam War.

Back then, Civil Rights advocates were smeared as dangerous and violent ███████.

Among students' most pressing demands to-day—beyond ending ████████ in ████—is *divestment* of their universities' financial ties to the military-industrial complex, echoing past U.S. student campaigns against South African apartheid. Such demands previously succeeded in the 1980s, the 2010s, and most recently compelled Brown and Rutgers Universities to negotiate actual divestments.*their*

Despite its universalist phrasing, the law exclusively protects one group by penalizing any expression "against Jews," legally equating criticism of Israel or Zionism with antisemitism.

It establishes a singular official philosophy: "*The International Holocaust Remembrance Alliance's working definition of antisemitism.*" This organization has faced repeated criticism for conflating antisemitism with critiques of Israeli state policies and blurring distinctions between antisemitism and anti-Zionism. Until now, their "███████*working definition*" carried no direct legal consequences. Now it does.

The law states: "*Antisemitism is increasing in the United States and is affecting Jewish students in K-12 schools, colleges, and universities.*" This is accurate. However, this resurgence stems not from ███████████

activism or leftist movements globally, but from resurgent neo-Nazi and far-right white supremacist groups expanding governmental influence—who, as in Europe and Latin America, typically support ███ at-any-cost. Observe libertarian movements in the U.S., Brazil, Argentina, Italy, France, Ukraine and elsewhere.

Similarly, the First Amendment's free speech protections again prove what they've always been since 1791: the freedom of white men, wealthy men, imperial slaveholders. When abolitionists attempted to exercise it in the 19th century, they faced harassment, persecution, imprisonment, and lynching.

"*Combating this hatred is a bipartisan national priority requiring a whole-of-government and whole-of-society* approach." Police spitting on Palestinian flags on campus, politicians declaring Palestinians should be erased from Earth, rabbis claiming Buddhists or those kneeling before Jesus deserve death as idolaters—none constitutes hate speech or incitement. The systematic de facto annihilation and harassment of Palestinians isn't hate speech because it isn't speech.

Beyond underground militia resistance—standard for any colonized people—Palestinians lack a formal military. If they defend themselves violently (a right recognized by the UN and common sense), they're terrorists. Moreover, they don't exist. They're fictional constructs invented by "hate speech" purveyors.

As Netanyahu's government members themselves state: Palestinians don't exist—they're Amalek's descendants, requiring the extermination of men and children per a divine command issued to current Defense Minister Ben-Gvir three millennia ago. As Golda Meir said, "*We cannot forgive them for forcing us to kill their children.*" But this is neither racism nor an attack on a human group due to their ethnic or religious origin. On the contrary, the law shields American politicians and the government ████████ of Israel from being accused of suppressing the existence of tens of thousands of children and other humans in Gaza because of Hamas—for some mysterious reason, Hamas's hostages never die under any bombardment ██████.

The law is an achievement of legislative creativity, immunizing one specific group of human beings while omitting others. All calls to exterminate Palestinians, repeated endlessly by authorities, journalists, and religious figures, are not considered and therefore not punishable. On the contrary, they are now protected from all criticism. Neither the International Criminal Court nor the International Court of

Justice nor any law can infringe upon the sacred and divine right of Israel to ███████ a hundred thousand people in less than a year in the name of self-defense.

For several generations now, any reaction to this divine right has been censored as terrorism. As Israel's ambassador Gilad Erdan said at the UN the day before: "*We always knew Hamas hides in schools. We didn't realize they're also at Harvard, Columbia, and many elite universities.*" Shortly after, Arkansas Senator Tom Cotton held a press conference denouncing the "little Gazas" on university campuses. Like Gaza, pro-Palestinian students suffered the violent repression of police and pro-Zionist groups.

That's why they must be punished there too. The new law specifies that its goal is "*to expand the power of the Secretary of Education*" to grant them freedom to punish those who do not understand what the Government understands. The law concludes with the following phrase, worthy of a religious figure interpreting sacred scripture: "*Nothing in this Act shall be subject to interpretation.*" A century ago in Italy, this went by the name of ███████.

When someone is offended by protests against the ███████ of 70 thousand people, more than half of them children and women, nearly all of them

(unjustly) unarmed, but is not bothered by the
███████████ of 70 thousand people, the answer defines
itself without further help.

The Nazis didn't just shut down the historic
Bauhaus architecture school, which they deemed corrupt—they also declared the Theory of Relativity false
because its author was Jewish, while banning thousands of books for being *anti-German*. Now
███████████. We continue moving closer to that
same surrealism.

From now on, in the Greatest Democracy of
the Free World, we'll have to become more poetic and
abuse metaphors, as in the time of Nero, who was re-
ferred to with the number 666 (his name in Hebrew
letters) because, though some freedom of speech existed, it was forbidden when it effectively challenged
the imperial power of the time.

WHAT HAVE WE LEARNED FROM THE STUDENTS?

ONE OF THE NATURAL MANIFESTATIONS of any social power fossilized at the apex of the social pyramid is the division of those below. The capitalist variation of this ancient law, *divide et impera*, lay in the explicit inoculation of racism and the demobilization, disarticulation, and demoralization of any social organization that wasn't the guild of millionaires—those who can stage capital strikes whenever they please (in the name of the sacred right to private property of their capital) and pressure entire populations with need and hunger every time they decide to do the same: unite to defend their individual rights, their class interests, their dignity as colonized peoples.

The massive protest movement of American students against the massacre in Gaza—which, to a significant extent, sparked uprisings in other Western countries—appears as a *paradoxical phenomenon*. At least, that's how journalists who consulted me on the matter have described it.

Like all paradoxes, it is a logic that seems contradictory: in the country whose citizens are known for their geopolitical ignorance, their disinterest—if not outright insensitivity—toward their own imperialist wars and blind patriotism, their addiction to consumption, and their militaristic and religious fanaticism, the student protests belong to a tradition that began in the 1960s with anti-war movements, continued in the 1980s with protests against South African apartheid, and later with various demands for divestment from the war industry, private prisons, and ecocidal pollution by the administrators of their powerful universities.

As in all cases, they were discredited as irresponsible, dreamy youth—when in fact, precisely those young people were the best-informed and bravest in their society, despite not coming from a group submerged in the violence of basic needs. This, too, isn't hard to explain: not only does non-commercialized knowledge, not only does the least corrupt idealism of youth account for this reaction, but no one can imagine a union of *homeless* organizing to demand better living conditions, not because they are productive but for the simple reason of being human beings.

But I believe there's another reason that explains this phenomenon, and it's likely one of the main causes. As I noted earlier, the division of those below has always been a weapon of domination for those above. I could dwell on countless crucial examples

from the last two centuries, but the rule is so funda-
mental that few would question it. One of its manifestations—demobilization—was   and   remains   an
unwritten yet deeply entrenched policy within capitalism itself: first, demobilization through the dismantling and demonization of social organizations like
labor unions. Second, through the consolation of
churches, which overwhelmingly supported or justified economic, political, and social power. Third,
through the only sacred secularization that was permitted: consumerism and the dogma of individual-
ism. Selfishness and greed, for centuries considered
sins among the communal Christians of the faith's
first three illegal centuries, and moral failings in most
ancient social philosophies, became sacred virtues by
the 16th century to appease and fuel the fever of the
new capitalist ideology.

But let's return to the specific case of American
students. Anyone who has been a student or professor
in the U.S. has a clear sense of campus life. Though
some come from the upper classes and don't need
scholarships or loans because their parents cover their
entire education, the vast majority borrow from their
own futures to pay the world's most expensive tuition.
Others, through luck or early merit, receive scholarships. In any case, despite being embedded in a

fiercely segregationist national and global system where class privileges and struggles are no less brutal, on campuses these differences fade almost to nothing. That's the first point.

The second point, equally contradictory to the rest of social reality, lies in the constant social, collective, almost familial interaction among university students. A large portion (sometimes a majority) live in campus housing. Those who don't might as well. In my classes, for example, barely ten percent come from the city where the university is located, despite Jacksonville having a million residents. Most hail from states as distant as New York or California and continents as varied as Europe, Latin America, Africa, and Asia. I'd be surprised if next semester's classes don't follow the same pattern. This wonderful diversity (true, the poor are a minority, but they exist thanks to scholarships) fosters a global human awareness absent from the provincial fanaticism of much of society—and better known abroad, since the ridiculous and absurd tends to spread and go viral more quickly.

The third point (though for these reflections it's actually the first) lies in how this lifestyle exposes young people not just to different ways of thinking through their classes, but to different lifestyles through coexistence with their international peers—

from sports distractions and park barbecues to some excessive parties in their fraternities and sororities with their extreme pranks. One day I arrived at my office at dawn and along the way encountered panties and bras hanging from a tree near the entrance of a building where I usually teach. Just youthful antics.

As a professor, I've served on various committees like student affairs, and though my criticism of the U.S. university system is that it's less democratic than Europe's or Latin America's since, for example, students don't vote, they nonetheless manage to organize themselves and demand what they consider just and necessary.

In other words, students aren't misinformed, demobilized, disorganized and intimidated as they'll become when they turn into cogs in the machine. This makes them *dangerous* to the system, which explains their powerful protests across 50 campuses nationwide for a human rights cause they deemed just, necessary and urgent.

The example of students whose only power lies in their unity must be understood with the seriousness it deserves. The political (economic and media) establishment understood this first—which is why they not only permitted violence against students but repressed them with irrational brutality, arresting 3,000 of them while none of the fascists who initiated the violence faced consequences.

A corollary is the urgent need for the rest of society to reorganize into groups and unions again—not just workers' unions but all kinds of associations, from grassroots political committees to neighborhood councils. This can be achieved using the very tools of division and demobilization wielded against them: digital technology.

We'll have a new world when individuals join different groups and assemblies—even virtual ones—to discuss, listen, propose, and feel belonging to something beyond the impoverished individuality of consumerism. If humans are selfish, we're no less altruistic. When we identify a just cause, we fight for it beyond our self-interest. Examples abound.

Will we relearn that humanity's common interest—the species' interest—is, at least in the long term, the individual's most important interest? In reclaiming this communal sense, this engagement, lies the salvation of both the individual and humanity.

Over time, this multiplicity of communities at different levels and with different interests will ensure that voluntary donations and taxes stop flowing to ultra-wealthy individuals who buy presidents, senators, armies and even global opinion. Because the rich don't donate—they invest. When they're not investing in politicians, judges or journalists, they're investing in the morality market. As a rule, not an exception, the rich always have personal motivations for "donating."

Humans are driven by self-interest and collective causes. There's no need to clarify which, in political and ideological terms, is the right and which is the left. In any case, both interests are human and must be considered in the equation that will make this anxious, violent, and dissatisfied species something better. For that to happen, the majority must cease to be a disposable, irrelevant class.

THE SAME FACTS. A NEW CONSCIOUS-
NESS?

"David lived in Philistine territory [Canaanite inhabitants of what is now Gaza up to the Jordan] *for a year
and four months (...) He devastated the region, leaving no
man or woman alive; he seized sheep, oxen, donkeys, camels, and garments, then returned to Achish. David left no
one alive to avoid bringing them to Gath, saying: 'Lest they
report against us and denounce us to the Philistines.' This
was David's conduct the entire time he lived in Philistine
territory."*

1 Samuel 27:7

I

IN 1995, I TRAVELED THROUGH LEBANON, Jordan, Palestine, and Israel on foot. Along the ruined roads, Palestinian children threw small stones at me, thinking I
was Jewish (*"Juif!"*). Jewish children spat at me and
said they would kill all Christians (finger to throat:
"you Christians, all"). But my enthusiasm and curiosity
outweighed any inconvenience. I was detained in several places, the last time for two hours at Tel Aviv airport; the agents couldn't understand how a poor

student (son of a Uruguayan carpenter, sleeping on the streets of Jordan and surviving on one machine-made ice cream a day in Jerusalem) could travel around the world in nine months. As Oriana Fallaci said, "[_____] *must be paying for the plane tickets of the poor who come to piss in our beautiful squares.*"

Shortly after landing in Rome, I learned that Yitzhak Rabin had been assassinated by a Jewish fanatic enraged by the peace talks. Since then, everything went from bad to worse. A year earlier, one week after hearing the biblical account of wiping out all the inhabitants of Amalek—a command given 3,000 years prior—Baruch Goldstein from New York massacred 29 Muslims in a Hebron mosque. Peter Beinart, an Orthodox Jew from *New Republic*, wrote that "*the wisdom of rabbinic tradition was declaring that we no longer know who Amalek is; this restricts the clear genocidal meaning of the biblical text.*" When Netanyahu claims to know who Amalek is, "*he's dismantling the moral framework created by Jewish tradition and affirming a biblical literalism alien to Judaism of the past two thousand years - and given his military power, it's terrifying.*"

But it's deceptive to reduce Israel's entire militaristic policy to one man or a ministerial cabinet that repeats the same need to "kill everyone, including children," because they'll become "*tomorrow's terrorists*" and, as if that weren't enough, accuses its critics of racism. An unsurpassable example of religious fanaticism combined with unchallengeable military power and media influence that's beginning to crack worldwide.

II

I'M TRANSLATING HERE THE LETTER from presidential candidate Jill Stein sent by mail to those of us closely following her political career in the United States, a rare bird in a system called *democratic* but hijacked by secret megacorporations like BlackRock, Vanguard and other sects.

Nothing Stein denounces is new, as many other media outlets, prisoners and humanitarian workers have reported similar abuses for years. When these reports were made, the Israeli government labeled the organizations as "terrorist groups" and their criticisms as *antisemitic* or "Hamas sympathizers." This was the case, for example, with the organization *Defence for Children International*, which includes Josh Paul, a U.S. State Department official. After a thorough study of allegations regarding the rape of a 13-year-old Palestinian boy in an Israeli prison in Jerusalem, the Israeli military raided their offices, seized all computers, and Tel Aviv declared the NGO a "terrorist entity."

Let's remember that in Israeli prisons there are 9,500 Palestinian detainees without due process, arrested under the criteria of those who accuse them of posting images or reports against the occupation or for throwing stones at war tanks. In no judicial system should minor prisoners be anything other than kidnapped children.

The CIA also has dozens of secret prisons around the world, where neither U.S. nor international law applies. Less secret but equally unpunished has been - and remains - Guantánamo, the place where all human rights are violated in Cuba without Havana or any other government in the world being able to include Washington on the list of "States that promote terrorism."

Stein concludes her letter with something I'm not sure can be considered obvious, but which is undoubtedly central to the conflict: "*Biden could end ALL of this right now with a single phone call. Instead, our government continues funneling weapons and cash to Israel.*"

III
Jill Stein's letter

is horror upon horror. Even as the Rafah border crossing with Egypt remains blocked by Israeli tanks and the siege tightens further around Gaza, a shocking new CNN report has surfaced today exposing a secret desert prison where Israeli Occupation Forces are torturing Palestinian detainees.

A graphic with a headline published on Friday, May 10, 2024 states: "Bound, blindfolded, in diapers: Israeli whistleblowers detail abuse of Palestinians in shadowy detention center."

Here's what we know: three Israeli whistleblowers have provided details and photographic evidence of psychological and physical torture, including ritual humiliation and dehumanization, inflicted upon illegally imprisoned Palestinian citizens in Israel's Negev desert.

The whistleblowers described prisoners having limbs amputated due to injuries from constant handcuffing and medical procedures performed by unqualified personnel, mentioning this prison is known as "paradise of hell."

The images shared by whistleblowers are too disturbing to publish here. This represents a shocking regression similar to what innocent Iraqis endured at Abu Ghraib prison when tortured by American forces

- torture exposed to the world exactly 20 years and 12 days ago.

We don't know the total number of Palestinians detained in facilities like Sde Teiman. What we do know is there are thousands (if not tens of thousands) arrested by the Israeli army from both Gaza and the West Bank. We don't know how many more secret prisons exist, and we can be certain we haven't yet heard the worst of the abuses.

It bears repeating that Biden could stop ALL of this right now with a single phone call. Instead, our government continues indiscriminately funneling weapons and cash to Israel.

Our government's ongoing and unconditional diplomatic cover for these horrors makes our country complicit in Israel's war crimes.

Stop the weapons and war aid. Impose an embargo on this monster. The world must act *now*.

In solidarity, Jill Stein

MYSTERIES AND QUESTIONS OF A BIBLICAL NEO-GENOCIDE

In May 2024, Israeli Knesset member Tally Gotliv stated in a parliamentary speech: "The U.S. threatens to stop sending us precision missiles. I have news for America: we have imprecise missiles! So instead of using one precise missile to take down one room or building, we'll use imprecise missiles to take down ten buildings. If they don't give us precision missiles, we'll use imprecise ones."

Eighty percent of Gaza has been destroyed by massive bombardment. Thousands remain missing under rubble. Thousands will die (indeed, are already dying) from starvation and preventable or treatable diseases, as international doctors report.

Meanwhile, Hamas's hostages are demanded as the condition and "final solution" to the conflict - as if saying that if someone kidnaps my family member, I have the right to kill a thousand or ten thousand residents of their neighborhood and call them "collateral damage." Hence one favored argument justifying repeated massacres is: "Why aren't U.S. students protesting Hamas's hostages?" This supposedly proves protestors are *antisemitic*, *pro-Hamas*, as U.S.

lawmakers and Israel's UN ambassador have claimed. Students are accused of caring more about some victims than others, necessitating hate-speech legislation, etc.

These accusations fail the most basic moral reciprocity test, but the answer to why students protest is simple:

They protest not about a single event on October 7, but about an ongoing, unrelenting massacre.

They protest the root problem, which began generations ago and has since poisoned the world.

They protest because they're unwilling participants in and resisters of what they consider immoral. Their money - taken from their future to pay for education, plus American taxes - goes not to Palestinian resistance but systematically and without limit to the Israeli military, accelerating this massacre and continued dehumanization of a people denied even protest rights, as years of evidence show.

They protest an apartheid more brutal than South Africa's, as victims have detailed and anyone can see in testimonial videos or reports from those Israelis and Jews not dehumanized by the religious, political and chauvinist extremism taught in schools and media.

They protest because they've realized that democracy and freedom for all resembles the proud phrase

"*We the People*," where "people" theoretically means everyone, but practically means just a small group in power within a system served by slaves.

They protest because 2,500 of them have been arrested for protesting while none of the anti-protest groups who started campus confrontations have faced similar consequences.

They protest because they're being threatened with blacklists by major corporations.

They protest because those who haven't been arrested for protesting yet have already been informed their faces are being recorded by cameras, by new AI systems and by old ideological surveillance systems.

They protest because they're not being allowed to protest.

Doesn't Israel have the right to defend itself?

Don't Palestinians have the right to defend themselves?

What about the hostages?

The human hostages or the subhuman hostages?

Currently there are 9,500 hostages in Israeli prisons, detained without due process. Many have died in these dungeons after years of confinement. As Jill Stein has acknowledged, it's estimated there are tens of thousands detained in secret prisons in Israel - tortured, humiliated, and amputated. Most aren't Gazan

Palestinians but rather the harvest of Israel's long tradition of arbitrary arrests in the West Bank. A large number are minors. Some Israeli soldiers have testified about the rapes and torture practiced in these prisons. Other organizations have denounced sexual assaults on detained minors, which the Israeli government later labeled as antisemitic or "terrorist groups."

In this latest escalation of violence that began with Hamas's October 7, 2023 attack (the latest chapter in Palestine's long history of violent occupation, displacement of its native population, brutalization, dehumanization and demonization oftheir resistance as "terrorists" - a story spanning generations), two major mysteries persist:

Questions: I

Why was a music festival organized just kilometers from the Gaza border?

Did the world's most powerful intelligence know nothing about Hamas's plans?

Why did the world's most heavily guarded border allow armed militants through to kill and take hostages, while the response took several hours and, when it came, didn't prevent kidnappings but rather killed its own citizens with airstrikes?

Wasn't this attack a perfectly designed excuse to finish "killing all the inhabitants of Amalek" and occupy a strategic point in the name of the famous "right to self-defense"?

Questions: II

Why has the indiscriminate destruction of Gaza through massive daily bombings costing millions produced "collateral damage" killing 40,000 innocents (two-thirds children and women) but supposedly no Israeli hostages?

Why doesn't Tel Aviv fear killing Israeli hostages when dropping bombs that wipe out entire neighborhoods?

Are they so sure none of the hostages are hidden there, being used as "human shields"?

Or do they not matter either, because the goal isn't their liberation but the continued dispossession of "Palestinian subhumans" by "the people of light"?

Does Israeli intelligence know their locations and avoid bombing those precise spots?

How is it possible that one of the world's most powerful intelligence agencies, operating with one of the world's most powerful armies, with no technical or moral restrictions, claims to have found empty non-existent tunnels, child terrorists, but can't locate a single hostage?

If all this bombing was conducted without endangering hostages, it can only mean Intelligence, the military, and Netanyahu's government know exactly where both hostages and captors are.

Why haven't they gone after them, instead dedicating themselves to massacring the population with weekly equivalents to October 7th for over seven months?

One needn't be a genius to answer these questions, but the answers are extremely dangerous. Or will inconvenient questions be criminalized too?

THE MASKS OF RACISM

EVERY HISTORICAL EVENT manifests in concrete situations, never abstract ones, creating the illusion of specificity about the forces behind it. Nobody loves or hates in the abstract, even when the objects of that love (a flag, a symbol) or hate (another flag, another symbol) stem from tribal imagination and social struggles over "semantic fields" and their ethical valuations. We analyzed this in the book*The Narration of the Invisible*, 2004.

Hate breeds hate and conveniently distributes it until racists become indistinguishable from the outraged. Nobody hates abstractly. Nobody kills abstractly. There's no hate without concrete victims. Even pilots viewing reality as a video game or drone operators thousands of kilometers away kill concrete human beings, with concrete perpetrators later hiding behind concrete lies beyond any script - as we've seen for at least three decades.

Yet if we take the broadest possible historical view and try to abstract these forces - these common factors in our time and in Pontius Pilate's - we'll see more than just the circumstantial and specific. This Platonic idea (that truth is the constant beyond the chaos of visible appearances) remains the foundation of all scientific reflection. Philosophy and the sciences—from chaotic economics to quantum physics—have been nothing else. As a character in Ernesto Sábato's work once said, the beauty lies in understanding that a falling stone and the moon that doesn't fall are the same phenomenon.

Contrary to appearances, racism against a specific group doesn't exist. There's no such thing as specific, inclusive racism. Racists don't hate just one race, ethnicity, or people. This confusion is another of those classic *strategic confusions* that serve racists by allowing temporary alliances for their cause. There may be white racism and black racism, Semitic racism and anti-Semitic racism, but a racist is someone sick in body and soul who hates everyone not belonging to their race or ethnicity—those imaginary constructs that, like all imaginary things, often wield more power than reality. A racist hates democratically and indiscriminately, though periodically they focus, distract themselves, and ultimately unleash all their hatred on another specific ethnicity. A Nazi doesn't hate only Jews. A Ku Klux Klan supremacist doesn't hate only Black people. An anti-Semite doesn't hate only Semites. A supremacist Zionist doesn't hate only

Palestinians. This isn't just theoretical observation or linguistic definition. It's observable throughout history and today. If someone defends the group targeted by their hatred, they immediately become an enemy and object of that hatred without reservation. Recently, The New York Times and CNN identified those inciting violence against pro-Palestinian protesters at U.S. universities. Among the pro-Zionist mobs were activists from the anti-Jewish far right, including at least one known anti-Semite, assaulting students protesting the massacre in Palestine—among them Jewish students and professors. Similar examples abound. I lack space here to mention even a fraction of that long list.

No, a racist doesn't hate only one specific group, though strategic confusion insists on presenting it that way. If the group embodying the racist's hatred disappeared from Earth, within hours they'd redirect their sickness onto another group. Nobody gets sudden diarrhea from using one particular bathroom. Any bathroom will do to relieve their incontinence.

Racism is likely an evolutionary pathology (perhaps with some unstudied *individual genetic* component, like psychopathy) that becomes entrenched and amplified through cultural elaboration, justifications, and rationalizations. In the 19th century, supremacist

rationalizations took the form of pseudoscientific racial theories (*collective genetics*) to justify colonialism,
plunder, and the global massacres perpetrated by pristine Northwestern democracies. In the 21st century, as
five thousand years ago, it's religious justification ar-
ticulated through messianic fantasies of each group,
led by its most pathological members—whom political systems invariably select, nearly always democratically, though never freely.

But history also shows that while racism is a universal curse, not all peoples have practiced it on the
same scale or with equal passion. Though not exempt
from terrible massacres promoted or justified by racism, Africa also provides many historical examples
where race was an irrelevant detail. The same can be
said of several Native American peoples. All savages
and underdeveloped... Nothing comparable to the
genocidal supremacism that Northwestern empires
practiced on an industrial scale. Some cultures are
sicker than others—and all, religious or not, are anti-
humanist.

Another chapter concerns who benefits from racism. It's not hard to observe, historically and today,
that racism—like religion—serves as an instrument of
power for ruling classes and elites. Enslaving the rest
of society, of humanity, becomes harder unless we first

convince ourselves we're superior by birth, entitled to special rights (to land, capital, life), and that exterminating or enslaving others constitutes "legitimate defense" of those *rights*. It's harder to enslave humanity if the rest of humanity doesn't explicitly or implicitly accept the colonizer's superiority, the oppressor's, the ruling class's: that the powerful, the unpunished, are more intelligent, more beautiful, more virtuous—and ultimately sacrifice themselves for our prosperity, as perfectly defined by Rudyard Kipling's poem "The White Man's Burden," promoted by Theodore Roosevelt and believed by nearly all the colonized. Nearly all—except the dangerous rebels pursued and crucified by soldiers of the colonial creole oligarchy.

One last point. Another function of racism, like sexism, is that despite being an imperial instrument of domination, it cleverly distracts detractors with legitimate grievances. The "culture war" (*The Narration of the Invisible*) has silenced challenges to the very order that racism serves. This was proven first in the U.S. and later elsewhere: in the 21st century, marches and protests against racial violence drowned out the consciousness of the sixties—that imperialism is the ultimate expression of racism, which itself is the ultimate expression of global domination through the most abstract god of all: money, whose religion is capitalism.

THE MYSTERY OF THE PALES-TINIAN PEOPLE

Palestinians never existed as a people when demanding human rights. Yet they existed as the Amalekites three thousand years ago—when it's time to massacre them.

PALESTINIANS ARE VERY strange people. Like subatomic particles in quantum physics—and according to Zionists—they possess the ability to exist in two different forms and places simultaneously. They exist and they don't.

They don't exist, yet we must "*kill them all,*" as Congresswoman Andy Ogles stated in Washington. "*Wipe all of Gaza off the face of the Earth,*" insisted Israeli Congresswoman Galit Distel Atbaryan; "*anything else would be immoral.*" Israel's Defense Minister Ben-Gvir was clear: "*Why so many arrests? Can't you just kill some? What will we do with so many detainees? It's dangerous for our soldiers.*" Israel's Finance Minister Bezalel Smotrich declared during a televised cabinet meeting: "*Rafah, Deir al-Balah, Nuseirat—all must be annihilated*" by God's command: "*You shall blot out the memory of Amalek from under heaven.*" On multiple

occasions, Prime Minister Benjamin Netanyahu, referring to Palestinians, repeated: "*Remember what Amalek
did to you, says our Holy Bible.*" Jewish Studies Professor Motti Inbari clarified Netanyahu's words: "*The biblical commandment is to utterly destroy all of Amalek.
And when I say utterly destroy, we're talking about killing
every single one of them—including babies, their possessions, their animals, everything.*" Likud member Danny
Neumann stated on television: "*In Gaza, everyone is a
terrorist. We should have killed 100,000 on the first day.
Very few in Gaza are human beings.*" Heritage Minister
Amihai Eliyahu proposed saving time by dropping an
atomic bomb on Gaza to fulfill the divine mandate.

In the first seven months of bombing, 40,000 men,
children, and women have been torn apart by explosives—not counting the disappeared, displaced, those
affected by famine, disease, irreversible mutilations,
and trauma. Yet from Netanyahu to President Joe
Biden, "*what Israel is doing isn't genocide; it's self-defense.*" If an armed group responds with violence (a
right recognized by international law), they're labeled
terrorists.

Those who refuse to be killed are terrorists. Those
who criticize the slaughter, like American students,
are terrorists. That's why in Europe and the U.S., protests against the Gaza massacre are violently

suppressed by militarized police, while Zionist violent attacks and Nazi parades receive respectful coverage. Because the powerful are that cowardly. Without powerful weapons, dominant media, and captive capital, they're nothing. A rigid arm for the fascist salute, and a trembling hand when questioning a massacre against defenseless humanity.

According to Zionists, Palestine never existed, and Palestinians never existed. Yet when, by Zionists' agreement with Hitler, these nonexistent Palestinians were expected to receive refugees from Nazism in Europe, the "nonexistent" were the overwhelming majority from the river to the sea. The ships arriving with "good genetic material," per Zionists, flew Nazi and British flags. When in 1947 the *Exodus*, carrying 4,500 refugees, approached Haifa, the British captain warned passengers they'd be arrested upon arrival because the British Empire didn't permit illegal immigration. "*If you resist arrest, we will have to use force.*" Upon reaching Palestine, refugees unfurled a banner reading: "*The Germans destroyed our families. Please don't destroy our hopes.*" Many remained detained, but a quarter-million entered Palestine—at least 70,000 illegally and by force.

Soon, some portion (we don't know how much) of Europe's victims became the victimizers of the

Middle East. The Zionist plan was backed by a campaign of terrorist bombings in Palestine—hotels blown up, police stations destroyed, hundreds of Palestinians massacred. Folke Bernadotte, the Swedish diplomat who facilitated the liberation of hundreds of Jews from Nazi concentration camps in 1945, was assassinated in Jerusalem two years later by Lehi, a Zionist group that called itself both terrorist and "freedom fighters." Lehi, a faction of another terrorist group, Irgun, had negotiated with German Nazis to establish Israel as a totalitarian state allied with Hitler's Reich. When this alliance failed, they tried with Stalin—with the same result. One of Irgun's (ex-)terrorists, Belarusian Menachem Begin, became Israel's prime minister in 1977. He was succeeded by one of Lehi's (ex-)terrorists, also Belarusian, Yitzhak Shamir, who became prime minister of Israel in 1983. Naturally, all changed their birth names.

Even before Israel's founding, Palestine's "nonexistent" inhabitants began being dispossessed to house refugees. Some Jewish refugees and some nonexistent Palestinians resisted eviction and exile, necessitating force—a special right to existence denied the rest of humanity—and the wrath of a merciless god feared by that same humanity. In early 2024, Israeli filmmaker Hadar Morag recalled: "*When my grandmother arrived here in Israel after the Holocaust, the Jewish Agency promised her a home. She had nothing—her whole family had been exterminated. She waited a long time, living in a tent under very precarious conditions. Then they took her to Ajami in Jaffa, to a beautiful beachfront house. She saw plates still on the table from the Palestinians who'd lived there before being expelled. She returned to the Agency and said 'Take me back to my tent—I'll never do to anyone what was done to me.' This is my inheritance, but not everyone made that choice. How could we become what once oppressed us? That is the great question".*

Some of the nonexistent Palestinians welcomed Jewish refugees when even the United States didn't want them, when even a president like Roosevelt sent nearly a thousand Jewish refugees back on the St. Louis to die in Europe's concentration camps. When the UN created two states in 1948 - Israel and Palestine - Israel decided that neither Palestine nor Palestinians existed, though to achieve this quantum miracle they had to steal their homes and lands, to displace them en masse and kill them with joy. All while lamenting the dirty work they had to do. "*We will never forgive the Arabs for forcing us to kill their children*," said Ukrainian immigrant and later Prime Minister Golda Meir. "*Palestinians never existed,*" she declared in 1969. "*I was Palestinian from 1921 to 1948 because I had a Palestinian passport*," she added a year later. As if saying Germany is Hitler and von Papen's invention or that Britain is Prussia because its anthem ("God Save the Queen") sounds like Prussia's ("God With Us").

References to Arabs and Palestinians as animals or subhumans are nothing new. It's a classic genre of Zionist supremacist racism that offends no one in the civilized imperial world. The same civilized world that can't tolerate hearing the word *negro,* but doesn't want to remember or acknowledge (much less compensate) the hundreds of millions of Black people massacred for their chosen peoples' prosperity. Just as the Nazis did with Jews, before massacring them without remorse they first needed to dehumanize the other.

In 1938, one of the leaders of the Zionist terrorist group Irgun, Belarusian Yosef Katzenelson, stated: "*We must create a situation where killing an Arab is like killing a rat. Let it be understood that Arabs are trash and that we, not they, are the power that will rule Palestine.*" In 1967, Israeli diplomat David Hacohen declared: "*They're not human beings, they're not people, they're Arabs.*" In November 2023, former Israeli ambassador to the UN Dan Gillerman said: "*I'm deeply puzzled by the world's constant concern for the Palestinian people and indeed for these horrible, inhuman animals who've committed the worst atrocities this century has seen.*" But if anyone notices this is pure, hardcore racism, they're accused of antisemitism - that is, of being *racist*.

Palestinians don't exist, but if they defend themselves, they're bad terrorists. If they don't defend themselves, they're good terrorists. If they let themselves be massacred, they're nonexistent terrorists. In Gaza, "*anyone over four years old is a Hamas supporter,*" former Mossad agent Rami Igra told state television. "*All civilians in Gaza are guilty and deserve to face Israel's policy of collective punishment, which prevents them from receiving food, medicine and humanitarian aid.*" He forgot to mention the systematic, indiscriminate bombings that every day decapitate and tear apart dozens of children, even those under four - who would presumably be subhumans, animals, rats, but not yet full-fledged terrorists.

Israel does have the right to defend itself, which includes every other human and divine right: right to displace, right to occupy, right to kidnap, right to imprison and torture without limits the minors of a nonexistent people.

Right to have no one criticize its rights.

Right to consider itself a superior people, by God's grace and by virtue of its special nature, of its superior spirit that the *goyim* could never attain.

Right to weep for the victims caused by this ethnic superiority and right to weep for the victims caused by the subhumans, the human rats.

Right to buy presidents, senators, representatives and editors-in-chief of other countries, like the United States.

Right to ruin the career and life of anyone daring to question any of these rights under accusations of antisemitism.

Right to massacre when deemed necessary.

Right to kill for fun when its soldiers are bored.

Right to dance and celebrate when ten tons of bombs massacre dozens of refugees in a camp full of starving people.

All because Palestinians both are and are not. According to this supremacist, messianic tale, Palestinians never existed as a people when demanding human rights. Yet they did exist as the Amalekites three thousand years ago, as inhabitants of a people who had to be displaced and exterminated "until not one remains" of those fictional, nonexistent beings.

Now, if you don't believe this tale, just repeat it endlessly and you'll understand it's the pure truth. A truth that if you dare question, you become a terrorist - just as Lot's wife became a pillar of salt for her audacity to disobey and look back where, they say, God was massacring a people for some of their members' sexual orientation.

BLOOD OLYMPICS

THE GREEK OLYMPICS WERE capable of interrupting wars to respect the sacredness of the sporting event. That truce, practiced since the 8th century BC, was called *ekecheiria*, through which both athletes and spectators from warring nations could travel safely to the same city where the games were organized and return, all under the protection of mutual honor. Athletes and attendees typically traveled from what are now Greece, Turkey, Italy, and even North Africa—distances that were longer and more costly then than a trip from Tierra del Fuego or Jakarta to Paris would be today.

Before becoming another commercial product in our capitalist civilization, the goddess of the Olympic Games was Nike, or *victory*, the cry of Marathon before he fell dead from his heroic effort. The *ekecheiria*, the truce, the suspension of all wars, was dedicated to Irene (Eirene), the goddess of Peace and sister of Dike, goddess of justice. Greek artists often depicted her as a beautiful young woman holding the child Ploutos in her left arm, even though Ploutos was not her son. Like the Statue of Liberty in New York, Irene also wore a crown and, in her right arm, raised a torch. Before becoming a new myth (the capitalist myth of *freedom of appropriation*), this gesture and the very concept of *freedom* had a very different meaning than it does today and, for thousands of years, was more or less the same across different cultures and continents: it was the gesture of a generous ruler stepping before the people to announce that, at that historical moment, the debts of the lower classes were forgiven. This gesture was not simply an act of generosity but an existential necessity for the continued functioning of a stagnant, declining society. Hence the idea of *freedom*, as many slaves and non-slaves were not free due to their debts—exactly as is the case today. As the great American economist and debt expert Michael Hudson explained, the phrase "*Lord, forgive us our sins*" comes from the oldest and most repeated plea: "lord, forgive us our debts," which is even found in the Bible—when translated without the religious dogmas of the time.

The Ploutos held by Irene, the goddess of peace, was (or is) the god of wealth, which, for the ancient world, made sense: from peace comes prosperity. In a tragic irony, today's so-called democracies are plutocracies—that is, they are expressions of the power of the wealthy, and it is they who multiply their riches with every war. For capitalist investors, the returns of peace are meager and slow.

After 2,700 years, we have finally become civilized, and things are different. Ploutos grew up and murdered Irene, which explains the abolition of the *ekecheiria* in the Olympic Games and in any other major sporting event, such as the World Cup. In 1992, there was an attempt to revive this ancient tradition, and the United Nations passed a resolution that, like many of its resolutions, is only applied when it benefits or doesn't bother the neighborhood bullies.

Now, major sporting events—not just the Olympics—have always been marked by high politics. Some cases from the last century are remembered in history books more for their political betrayals than for their sporting achievements.

After winning everything, Uruguay refused to participate in the 1934 World Cup in Italy as a protest against European arrogance, which complained that the first World Cup, hosted by Uruguay, was too far from the center—a situation that reminds me of the joke my dear father used to tell me: "*you come here instead—you're closer.*" Uruguay had traveled to the Olympics hosted in Europe—Paris 1924 and Amsterdam 1928—and won both, when those tournaments were the world championships where each country sent its best, not alternate teams or age-limited squads as they do today.

For France 1938, Uruguay protested again because the Europeans broke their promise to rotate the World Cup by continent (the hosting rights should have gone to Argentina, where Uruguay remains a favorite to this day), and to uphold the boycott against fascism, then led by Hitler and Mussolini. Additionally, Uruguay was the first national team to compete in international tournaments with a Black player—an ethical and political statement that unsettled many, including some Latin American countries.

No coincidence, Italy went on to win that World Cup until the tournament was suspended due to war, and when it resumed in Brazil, Uruguay won again with the famous Maracanazo, a national myth woven into the psychological DNA of that small, sparsely populated country.

Something similar could be said of the 1978 World Cup in Argentina. Uruguay did not participate, not for political reasons but due to its own failure in the qualifiers—though the refusal to call up its best overseas players for the qualifiers might have been due to the military dictatorship at the time, but that's just a footnote for football history experts.

The 1978 World Cup was a gift for the genocidal Rafael Videla, who did not hesitate to pressure his own players in training, foreign teams (such as Peru's), and rushed to take the spotlight when Argentina achieved its first world title—a very different achievement from 1986. It was a political-sporting celebration amid the massacres and disappearances of a fascist regime that used the championship as Mussolini had used the 1934 World Cup, Hitler the 1936 Olympics, and, in 1938, FIFA's World Cup, in the spirit of *Die Europa über alles*—Europe above all, Europe first.

Future historians will likely say something similar about the 2024 Paris Olympics.They will be remembered as the Olympics of genocide, under different names. None of the ongoing wars have prompted any *ekecheiria* (truce) - quite the opposite. In the media age, the powerful always wait for some major global distraction to commit their worst atrocities. As during the years of Nazism and fascism, the only effect has been to marginalize those not favored by central political power - like Russia - while inviting Israel to participate amid one of the worst genocides in recent generations, compounded by the fact that it is not only rooted in explicit, undisguised racism (ironically, sports remain where we see the strongest resistance to racism) but is being carried out with the weapons, money, and media blessing of the same hegemonic center that, as during slavery, beats its chest while proclaiming itself the champion of Democracy, Freedom, and Human Rights.

Three moral categories in which they win no medals—yet they pin them on themselves anyway.

THE EMPIRE OF DENIAL CLOSES ITS EYES AND BELIEVES

"PROFESSOR," A STUDENTsaid to me, "take a gamble—tell us who's going to win tomorrow."

"Trump."

I'd already said it across several media outlets, but partisan politics don't interest me in my lectures.

"Every poll says Kamala wins. Why would she lose?"

"Because of Gaza. You can't hide the sun with one finger."

Hours after the election results came in, major networks from CNN to Fox News began digesting Donald Trump's victory. The most prominent figures seemed to agree on three issues that had hurt the Democrats: 1. The economy; 2. The immigration crisis; 3. The Middle East conflict.

In other words: wallets, racism, and morality. On all three points, we see the manufactured ideas and sentiments of those very networks' propaganda:

1. The domestic economy isn't doing well, but let's acknowledge this isn't due to any particular administration—it stems from a much larger structural problem, from the legalized corruption of corporations that have bought everything (politicians, media) to keep accumulating the wealth (surplus value) they've been wresting from the working and middle classes. Since 1975, the working class has transferred $50 trillion (twice China's GDP) to the top 1%.

The other economic factor is Washington's loss of global hegemony and dictating power, which hasn't just worsened its natural aggressiveness but has met competition it refuses to accept. Yet if we limit ourselves to comparing administrations, we see GDP grew less under Trump than under Biden. True, there was a pandemic—but the same logic applies when praising lower fuel prices during the previous term, caused by drastically reduced traffic.

2. There is an immigration *issue* at the southern border, but not a *crisis*. That's a media fabrication, fueled by politicians who benefit from demonizing the voiceless weak who lack lobbies to pressure or buy them. Generally, undocumented immigrants aren't criminals—they reduce crime. They don't live off state services; they contribute taxes through consumption and wages, paying into Social Security for others' benefit. They don't steal jobs—they do work citizens won't, greasing the economy's wheels.

Trump claims, "Illegal immigrants are criminals flooding in unchecked." He threatened Mexico with tariffs if it doesn't stop drug trafficking, omitting that his country is the root problem—not just in consumption but in drug and arms distribution. As documented, criminals, genocidaires, and terrorists live free and legal in Florida, bankrolling his party.

3. While Americans often vote with their wallets, some (though a minority, numbering millions) vote with deep moral conviction. This was the case with Gaza's genocide, which Democrats tried to silence to avoid discussing the weapons and tens of billions sent to Israel in one year to massacre tens of thousands of children under rhetoric like "Israel's right to defend itself" or, as Bill Clinton put it, "because King David was there 3,000 years ago." Or candidate Harris, deflecting Gaza questions with nasal arrogance: "I'm speaking." The administration ignored mass student protests—violently suppressed—citywide marches, truckers' boycotts...

Then, when backlash voting emerged, the same media that erased Gaza's slaughter scrambled to explain the electoral disaster by *demoting morality to third place, framing it as "Middle East crisis"—never saying Gaza, Palestine, or genocide*. Not even *massacre*.

This genocide metastasizes across the Middle East, another stop on the Ring of Fire (Ukraine, Syria,

Palestine, Iran, Taiwan) ignited by the friction of the Western Alpha Male encircling the awakened Dragon.

Rather than negotiating and benefiting their people through global cooperation, the Alpha Male is focused on eliminating the competition. This metaphor, drawn from a wolf pack led by a dominant male, is now embraced by right-wing ideologues. They forget that when an alpha male ages and faces a younger rival, it often ends in mortal conflict.

In 2020, Democrats won Wisconsin and Michigan, two states with significant Arab populations. This time, Republicans took both. Yet Palestinian-American Representative Rashida Tlaib (Michigan) retained her seat with 70 percent of the vote, and Ilhan Omar (Minnesota) won with 75 percent.

This was less a vote for Trump (who had lost the election four years prior for some reason) than a vote against Harris and the Democrats—an angry, hopeless protest. This electoral system is a legacy of slavery, and the political-media apparatus has been bought by the tech and financial corporations that truly govern this country. Larry Fink, CEO of BlackRock (a firm managing wealth equivalent to five times Russia's GDP), put it plainly: "*It doesn't matter who wins; Harris or Trump will both be good for Wall Street.*"

It's a money funnel: funds flow from parties to media for advertising and promotion. The same dollar buys politicians and press at different stages. Presidents handle the circus—stoking passions, especially racial and gender divisions. No better strategy exists to obscure class issues. Racism remains the most effective tool to mask our deep-seated class problem, including its global manifestation: imperialism.

Now we'll have a president convicted in 34 cases, one who boasted about being "smart" for dodging taxes. But cleverness alone isn't enough. You need a populace dulled by identity divisions, individuals *alienated* by the same tech giants dominating economy, politics, and geopolitics.

This isn't hard for a people conditioned to prioritize belief over facts. A people trained in churches to shut their eyes and *replace reality with desire* until reality bends. For the religious mindset, narrative truth outweighs objective truth: "*In the beginning was the Word...*"

From there, it's a short step—sometimes no step at all—to applying the same intellectual habits when moving between temples of power: banks, stock exchanges, television studios, political parties.

MEDIA JUSTIFYING ENDS II

ON JANUARY 9, 2025, DAYS after rejecting a paid ad condemning Gaza's genocide for using the word "genocide," The New York Times published "*Historians Condemn Israel's 'Scholasticide.' The Question Is Why.*" The American Historical Association had overwhelmingly voted to condemn Israel's bombing and total eradication of Gaza's schools and universities, alongside the killing of professors and students under tons of explosives. The featured article questioned the condemnation's rationale and accused universities of being *politicized*.

Days earlier, CNN, the anti-Trump network, pondered his expansionist proposals: "*Trump is grappling with national security issues; he must confront a world reshaped by China's rise… Trump's musings about terminating the Panama Canal Treaty reflect concerns over foreign powers invading the Western Hemisphere. This isn't new—it's been a historical constant since the 1823 Monroe Doctrine, when European colonialists were the threat. The issue persisted through Cold War communist fears. Today's usurpers are China, Russia, and Iran…*" Invasion, threat, usurpers... The same hypocritical journalism, ever complicit in genocidal, kleptocratic power.

For Latin America, the usurper has always been the United States. It was journalist John O'Sullivan who crafted the Manifest Destiny myth to justify dispossessing and massacring native peoples westward and southward—always cloaked in God's love for one ethnicity: the cannon's owner. In 1852, O'Sullivan wrote: "*This continent and its adjacent islands belong to whites; blacks must remain slaves...*"

When President James Polk fabricated an excuse to invade Mexico and steal half its territory, he staged a false-flag attack. "*It's time to spread freedom to other lands,*" he declared, meaning the reintroduction of slavery to a country that had outlawed it. His soldiers—Generals Ulysses Grant, Zachary Taylor, and Winfield Scott—admitted the sham. General Ethan Hitchcock wrote: "*We have no right being here. The government sent us to provoke Mexicans, creating a pretext for war so we can seize California.*"

The new mass press of that era, enabled by rotary press technology, became the primary *fake news* instrument, rallying thousands to invade Mexico and—as generals like Scott reported—to murder, plunder, and "*rape women before their own children and husbands.*"[8]Apparently, the United States wasn't sending its best men. On June 16, 2015, Trump was celebrated as he launched his presidential campaign by declaring that "*Mexico is sending people with problems... They're rapists.*"

When in 1846 Polk learned of a minor incident in Mexican territory, he rushed to Congress and reported: the invader "*has shed American blood on American soil.*" Lincoln, who had opposed the war (Ulysses Grant would call it "the rotten war"), was forced to withdraw from politics for years. Nothing silences criticism more effectively than warlike patriotism.

The same pattern continued for 150 years. The myth of the sinking of *the Maine* in Cuba was invented by yellow journalism, the business of Joseph Pulitzer and William Hearst. Years later, media mogul Hearst defended Hitler and accused F.D. Roosevelt of being a communist. The press portrayed Hitler as a patriot, just as it now portrays Netanyahu as an instrument of God.

In 1933, the most decorated general of his generation, Smedley Butler, wrote: "*The flag follows the dollar*

---

[8] Majfud, Jorge. *The Savage Border: 200 Years of Anglo-Saxon Fanaticism in Latin America.* Rebelde Ed., 2021.

and the soldiers follow the flag... Our wars have been planned by nationalist capitalism. I served in the Marines for 33 years as the muscle for Wall Street and big business... I was a capitalist gangster..." They didn't imprison him for his thought crime (as they did socialist candidate Eugene Debs for opposing WWI); they used a more common tactic: discrediting the military hero as psychologically troubled.

Johnson and Kissinger also invested millions in the press to support the genocidal Vietnam War with massive bombings and chemical weapons. By then, the CIA's Operation Mockingbird had already injected Latin America's major newspapers with *fake news* and editorials written in Miami. They did the same with U.S. media—books, literary criticism, and films. The ideological police served corporate interests while leaving hundreds of thousands massacred just in Central America, all in the name of *national security* that produced strategic insecurity.

Before the massive 2003 Iraq invasion (which left one million dead, millions displaced, and the Middle East in chaos), we published in marginal countries' newspapers about the illogic of its justification. But the hegemonic press convinced Americans the war drums spoke truth. The New York Times endorsed the invasion as patriotic "national security." Again, patriotism justified legal censorship (*Patriot Act*) and social harassment of critics. Media couldn't show soldiers returning in coffins, let alone hundreds of thousands of massacred Iraqi civilians—this collective cowardice only profited the usual merchants.

Years after George W. Bush and his puppet, Spanish PM José María Aznar, admitted the invasion's justifications were false ("intelligence failure"), most Fox News viewers still believed the lie debunked by its perpetrators—they'd been trained since childhood to believe against all evidence as if it were divine virtue.

Major media outlets selling themselves as *independent* and *guardians of democracy* depend not just on wealthy advertisers but billions from corporations and lunatics like Elon Musk who donate to political parties. A perfect business: *the same dollar that buys politicians in campaigns buys the media promoting them*. Media are part of this plutocratic dictatorship, their work (no different from priests giving sermons in churches and cathedrals funded by nobles) being to invent a reality contrary to facts—complicit with the great power of money, imperialism and racism. All in the name of democracy, international law and diversity.

As we formulated in $P = d.t$, the West will intensify censorship of critics simply because its *power* declines as its *tolerance* does. Since classical Greece, free speech has been a luxury of empires unthreatened by criticism.

BOMBS WITH MUCH LOVE

NIKKI HALEY ARRIVED IN ISRAEL on Sunday, May 26, 2024—one day before the Rafah massacre (one of many in preceding months). According to media headlines, Nikki traveled officially with humanitarian purposes.

Before taking a breather, she inspected the weapons that her country, the United States, provides to Benjamin Netanyahu's government. The latest check, approved weeks earlier by the U.S. Congress, was for $27 billion—1.5 times Palestine's entire economy.

Thanks to this new aid—adding to the annual transfer of nearly four billion dollars—Israel could accelerate the massacre of men, children and women in Gaza, the world's and history's largest prison. Of course, those who call this a massacre or genocide are antisemitic, which is why it's necessary to clarify that this is actually "Israel's legitimate right to defend itself against those who want to attack Israel and deny its right to exist."

In recent months, Netanyahu and his collaborators, with the (firm, complicit, convinced) support of the majority of Israel's population, have killed 40,000 of these prisoners (approximately half of them children; maiming and traumatizing for life over a million defenseless inhabitants) whom they consider animals or subhumans undeserving of life. Anyone who disagrees with killing all Palestinians is automatically labeled racist. If they were dogs or cats, the perpetrators would be condemned for animal cruelty. But no—Palestinians/Arabs "are rats," as defined by the founding members of the terrorist groups that established this racist, supremacist mentality, like Irgun and Lehi before the UN invented the State of Israel: *"We must create a situation where killing an Arab is like killing a rat. Let it be understood that Arabs are trash, and that we—not they—are the power that will rule Palestine,"* echoed more recently by former Israeli UN ambassador Dan Gillerman, who called Palestinians *"horrible, inhuman animals."*

Photos showed Nikki—ever so devoted to family values—writing on one of the bombs used hours later to kill dozens of innocent children:

"Finish them. USA loves Israel. Forever.
Nikki Haley"

Nikki Haley (born Nimarata Nikki Randhawa, daughter of Indian immigrant parents) was governor of South Carolina and the second-highest-voted candidate for the Republican presidential nomination.

Until recently, she was a contender for the Trump-Haley ticket in the upcoming election. In 1996, young Nimarata Randhawa married soldier and businessman Michael Haley and later converted to Christianity, the religion of love.

TERRORISTS?

NOVEMBER 2019. One of the thousands of children kidnapped by Israel's military. Currently, 9,500 Palestinians are imprisoned in Israel without due legal process for offenses like insulting officers, posting photos, social media comments, or throwing stones at tanks. For decades, international organizations (like Josh Paul, a former U.S. State Department official) have denounced the abuse and sexual violence against Palestinians—many of them minors—in Israeli prisons. The organizations exposing these crimes were labeled *terrorists*.

THE UNCIVILIZED CAN LEARN TO FARM

"Uruguay plans to 'bring some young Palestinians from the West Bank' for agricultural training under a FAO program, said Lubetkin"

(Channel 12, Uruguay, June 6, 2025)

ON MONDAY, MAY 12, 1919, the UK Secretary of State for War—future prime minister and WWII hero Winston Churchill—wrote about his own gassing of Arab protesters and rebels:

"I do not understand this squeamishness about the use of gas. At the Peace Conference, we have firmly upheld its retention as a permanent method of warfare... I am strongly in favor of using poisoned gas against uncivilized tribes. The moral effect would be so good that the loss of life would be minimized. It is not necessary to use only the most deadly gases: gases causing great inconvenience and spreading terror would also be fitting..."

Of Hindus, he said they were animals who worshiped elephants. True to form, he was directly and knowingly responsible for the famine that killed millions in Bengal in 1943, shortly before he signed an alliance with Stalin in Iran to fight Nazism.

These words from the British hero and champion of freedom and human rights, these supremacist ideas and actions, were neither novel nor scandalous at the time. Racist supremacy and messianism, like O'Neill's *Manifest Destiny* and Kipling's *White Man's Burden*—which in the 19th century justified slaughtering "uncivilized peoples" and "inferior races"—were the precursors to Hitler and Nazism. Hitler plagiarized entire passages from Madison Grant for *Mein Kampf* and thanked him for the inspiration. Nazism's popularity in countries like England and the U.S. was widespread, especially among wealthy businessmen and powerful politicians—until they started losing WWII, whereupon Nazi criminals were suddenly reduced to a handful of madmen rather than a complicit, cowardly mass of beautiful, superior amnesiacs.

A hundred years later, the history of suppressing uncivilized peoples, inferior races, and God-cursed nations is a thousand times worse—yet, as then, it's treated as no great matter. But the real-time information available today is also a thousand times greater, so the responsibility and shame (or shamelessness) must likewise multiply a thousandfold.

Today, Uruguay is one of those examples that fail to rise to tragedy solely due to its military and propagandistic inability to do much harm. Not because we're a superior people, as your government so kindly insists on making clear with its own example. Which doesn't exempt us from the shame of cowardly denial or moral wavering in the face of contemporary history's most tragic events. Cowardice and denial from which thousands of Uruguayans who don't tremble before current fascists exempt themselves—those who terrorize with total impunity from right to left, in that order.

After Uruguayan president Yamandú Orsi rejected his party's request (the left-wing coalition Frente Amplio) to define the massacres in Gaza as *genocide*, he defended himself by saying he's about actions, not words, and prefers not to speak about "the war" but rather provide "concrete solutions," like sending powdered milk and rice to Gaza... The Israeli embassy in Uruguay labeled Frente Amplio's criticism of the Gaza genocide as "expressions of disguised hatred" and warned of "dangerous conse-quences." B'nai B'rith called FA's brief statement "a grave moral failure."

Due to prior criticism from artists and left-wing activists regarding his government's hesitations, the president again tried to douse the fire with more fuel. In a new statement to newspapers, he said he condemned the "military escalation" and that Netanyahu's offensive "fuels antisemitism" and creates "weariness" among "important sectors" of the Israeli people.

It's quite obvious that the Zionist genocide can fuel, among other things, antisemitism, since it's always been the same Zionists who—for political, geopolitical, and ideological reasons—have strategically conflated and identified Zionism with Judaism (like equating the KKK with Christianity). Thus, even the hundreds of thousands of Jews who actively oppose Palestinian massacres and apartheid in Israel can end up being victims held responsible for something they condemn.

But what about the hundreds of thousands of massacred, mutilated, traumatized, and starved Palestinians? Aren't they the direct victims of the hatred and violence that insists "there are no innocents in Gaza, not even children," thereby justifying exterminat-ing them before they become "terrorists"? Could it be that the European settlers who claim descent from a man named Abraham who lived 4,000 years ago in what is now Iraq are the real antisemites? A man who first had a child with his slave at his infertile wife's request. But the son of Abraham and the slave produced the Arab lineage. Since something went wrong, Sarah had her son at age 90 by the Lord's miracle—the one who produced the Israeli lineage (according to the same tradition that identifies those Israelis from 3,000 years ago with today's), an upgraded version of his brother's race. But let's drop this surreal line of reasoning that's only obvious to perpetually entranced fanatics.

The mere idea of sending milk and rice to Gaza under the slogan "actions, not words" hides either profound ignorance of what happens to humanitarian aid in Palestine or, more likely, denialism and a well-known fear of criticizing the powerful party committing genocide—let's say *massacre*, so as not to offend the sensibilities of the killers and their apologists.

Of course, if you mention it, the automatic argument is "I haven't seen you condemn the October 8 attack." Which is false and paradoxical, since it's always said by those who never have and never will condemn the repeated massacres and systematic human rights violations against Palestinians and other neighbors since World War II, when the same Zionists proudly identified themselves as terrorists.

Uruguay's foreign minister, Mario Lubetkin (former Institutional Communication Director of FAO for Latin America), has stepped in to douse the fire (now a blaze) of criticism from his political base by announcing plans to allow "some young Palestinians from the West Bank" to come to the country for training in sustainable agriculture. In another radio program, he claimed Palestinian youth could "think about the day after" by becoming *entrepreneurs* and starting their own *start-ups*.

The day after what? Why do we, the Western masters, have to tell them what they must do to civilize themselves—how to indoctrinate themselves and adapt to progress and submission to Anglo-Saxon capitalism? Of course, exile them again, far from their land and their own sovereign decisions as individuals and as a people.

Beyond the Uruguayan foreign ministry's troubled conscience, many don't understand or imagine that Palestine has thousands of bilingual professionals and academics whose schools and universities were bombed to rubble. In Israel they're considered beasts of burden, and in the West they think they can teach them to plant olive trees.

In early 2024, I met with International Affairs officials at my U.S. university to propose creating "humanitarian scholarships" for students affected by armed conflicts. Although the idea was well received, it sank under donor apathy. But what a great idea— taking Palestinians out of Palestine to teach them to cultivate other lands! How had no one thought of it before? It's not about giving scholarships to youth who lost everything under bombs so they can prepare and wage an international struggle for their people's sovereignty, but so they can learn to farm land—other lands that have nothing to do with their own, which they know like the back of their hand and have cultivated for thousands of years in more than sustainable ways.

Where's the tiresome mantra we Western professors hear at toxic frequency about the need to "train world leaders"? Every time I criticize this colonialist slogan in meetings, many struggle to understand me.

Displacing Palestinian youth to learn "sustainable agriculture" in Uruguay is such a great idea that it resembles the "Final Solution" that members of Natadasco's cabinet—and most Israelis—talk about so much. According to a Haaretz poll, 82% of Israelis support the forced expulsion of Palestinians from Gaza.

OPEN LETTER

What Are You Afraid Of?

Those who remain silent today out of fear or convenience will claim tomorrow they were always against the genocide. Precisely when saying so serves no purpose except, once again, their personal interests.

Mr. President of Uruguay, Yamandú Orsi,
Madam Vice President Ana Carolina Cosse,
Mr. Foreign Minister Mario Israel Lubetkin,
Madam Defense Minister Sandra Lazo,
Ladies and Gentlemen of God's Embassy:

I WANT TO BELIEVE THAT HUMAN Rights, when not used as an excuse to invade a country or exercise hegemonic power for some empire, are not bound by partisan ideology. However, given Uruguay's and Latin America's tragic history, I find it appropriate to address some of you as left-wing men and women—people for whom this affiliation once meant commitment not just to ideas but to humanist values. Those same values that yesterday's neoliberal right covertly denied and that its unrecognized offspring, fascism, now proudly scorns: the values of equality, social justice, solidarity, tolerance for differing ideas, and intolerance toward the racist, sexist, classist, and imperialist morality of today's slaveholders.

In Uruguay, particularly, the left-wing men and women who resisted the dictatorship made Human Rights a non-negotiable banner—to the point of being accused and despised for it.

Now, what is the difference between supporting Uruguay's military dictatorship and supporting the genocide in Palestine? Both were and are imperialist brutalities, but the latter is a thousand times greater in deaths, massacres, amputations, trauma, torture, starvation, and disappearances. The latter, beyond being ideological, is profoundly racist and centuries older.

Foreign Minister Lubetkin: In dismissing a resolution from the Broad Front regarding the genocide in Gaza, you've summarized the thinking and values of this new government of disguised leftists, who increasingly abandon their ideals in the name of a pragmatism that, as always, serves the interests of the powerful: "*Political activism is one thing, governing is another; we are managing the government.*"

Didn't you feel even a hint of shame with such arrogance coming from someone who isn't even from the FA nor elected by the people? It reminded me of Nixon when he decided to remove Allende because Chileans had voted "*irresponsibly*." The same arrogance and contempt that explains the rest of the Palestinian tragedy and that of many other peoples without powerful secret agencies.

When questioned about Uruguay's (your government's) decision to purchase weapons from Israel, Minister Sandra Lazo responded with predictable shallowness: "*We'll buy (weapons) from whoever offers the best prices and quality. Uruguay has no enemies.*" Words and philosophy of neutrality in the face of barbarity, hidden behind pro-business pragmatism that was the norm in the 1930s to justify dealings with Hitler and, more recently, with the fascist regimes of Pinochet, Videla, and dozens of other mercenary dictators of the old global genocidal imperialism. Which, in the case of a former member of the guerrilla Marxist group MPP like yourself, remains a multilayered paradox.

Until yesterday, we still held some hope, but Vice President Cosse, known for an intellectual clarity rarely seen in current governments, dashed it completely when she refused to condemn the genocide in Gaza, adopting the silences, hesitations, and adjectives of President Orsi, recycling "tremendous" into "tragedy" to say nothing, do nothing, point to nothing and no one: "*I believe in peoples' self-determination... the Israeli people must find their path, like all peoples of the world, and I will respect that to the letter.*"

And what of the right to self-determination of the colonized, the victims of apartheid, the tens of thousands of massacred children, the executions for sport, the famine engineered without pretense and with ever fewer excuses?

Does this *left* truly feel better standing with supremacists and imperialist bombings?

Why does their conscience always waver when asked about Israel, only to breathe relief when journalists return to safer topics like child poverty and others' corruption?

What distinguishes this Latin American "left" from the genial pro-genocide, pro-imperialist progressives like Barack Obama and Kamala Harris?

When I worked in Mozambique alongside some Europeans, or traveling through Germany, I was always struck by how no one ever had a father or grandfather who was a Nazi. Regarding Uruguay's dictatorship, we were harsh in our criticism of collaborators and relentless with those who participated in torture and disappearances. Not so with those who had to remain silent because their lives and their children's depended on it.

That's not the case today. Those who remain silent now out of fear or convenience will claim tomorrow they were always against the genocide. Just when saying it serves no purpose, except, once again, for their personal interests.

The moral weakness in this case is infinitely worse. At least politicians, businesspeople, and denialist employees understand their positions or benefits depend on their complicit silence. At least let it be simple self-inflicted cowardice. There must be some reason beyond just classic excuses of Nazi genocidaires like "they are rats we must exterminate" and "we have the right to defend ourselves." Or from more recent genocide apologists, shamelessly repeating on Uruguayan public television that "there are no innocents in Gaza," or that "God gave us special rights three thousand years ago," and all that criminal rhetoric which the poor in spirit—who don't belong to the club—worship in temples, fearful of a hell that doesn't exist, according to the very creator of the Universe.

Uruguayans, the European Charrúas like Tabaré (the William Tell of the Switzerland of the Americas), who with some justification take pride in their democratic civility, have also given Latin America, from the left, lackeys like OAS Secretary Luis Almagro. Now we confirm this new tradition of what Malcolm X called "the house negro"—the slave, zealous guardian of his masters.

Esteemed elected and unelected (but appointed) members of the government:

Even if this administration becomes the most successful in history, no amount of chlorine in the world will wash away the shameful stain of its complicit stance toward the genocide in Palestine.

It will remain stamped
on the indelible memory
of all the annals
of history.

Of course, we can all err a thousand times with complex ideas, but one need not be a genius to have clear moral principles. Neutrality is the hallmark of cowards. A double cowardice when trying to justify it with dialectical stammering.

Take a minute of silence and reflect on what the greatest Uruguayans in history would say, from José Artigas to Eduardo Galeano, to name just two. The list of the worst, now in history's garbage dumps, is longer, but I don't recommend taking it as reference, much less continuing to expand it.

How history will judge us is painfully obvious but irrelevant right now. Those who still believe God created the Universe and Humanity only to incite one people to exterminate others will disagree, but with fanatics, no reasoning is possible.

What matters now is acting on the most basic moral principles, scorning fear of blacklists and fewer deals. If something only serves our personal or sectarian interests, it surely isn't moral.

Can we, the humans down here, expect any reaction from you, even if it's *too little, too late*?

July 2025

THERE IS SOMETHING THAT CANNOT BE BOUGHT OR SOLD, AND THAT'S WHY IT IRRITATES SO MUCH

WHEN THE UNITED STATES HAD SLAVES in shackles, it presented itself as a model of democracy. Even today, some insist it has never had a dictatorship.

South Africa's *apartheid* was defended by Ronald Reagan as a bastion of freedom in that continent full of Blacks prone to socialism, while Nelson Mandela occupied London and Washington's lists of "dangerous terrorists."

How is it possible that Israel, another *apartheid* regime according to all international human rights organizations and many Israelis, is defined as a democracy? A brutal regime, licensed to kill and massacre at will, armed with all the foreign billions in weapons and high-tech, weeping as if it were the universal victim.

What decent mind can accept that while tens of thousands of children are massacred, it's insisted that they—and all the children still starving, traumatized, and limbless—must die, and as if that weren't enough, they are fawned over by the trembling (*quivering*) leaders of the world's right and left?

I have a collection of cowardly threats (*bans*, blacklists), none of which frighten me, but I also have the solidarity of countless decent Jews who refuse to be corrupted by that fanatical, racist, supremacist ideology.

I'll repeat it a thousand times. They can kill as many humans as they want, they can threaten the billions on this planet who protest this barbarity, but they will never kill the dignity of others—the dignity those well-armed, fawning genocidal cowards never had.

History has a septic tank reserved for them just around the corner.

www.ingramcontent.com/pod-product-compliance
Lightning Source LLC
Chambersburg PA
CBHW032106280326
41933CB00009B/762